Hope these reflections endear you to my feelings about life here on the Neuse River —

Warmest regards,
Ben Casey
3/1/01

MAMA ALWAYS SAID...

...A LITTLE SOUTHERN WISDOM
FROM BACK ROADS, CREEKS AND RIVERS

D1637395

BEN CASEY

In Appreciation:
Edwina Woodbury and the editors and designers at
The Chapel Hill Press have nursed this project along
with both the patience and the enthusiasm essential
to doing the job right.
Simply saying "thank you" at the front of the book
is so inadequate . . . so . . . as Elvis would say,
"Thank you very much".

ISBN Number   1-808849-30-5

Manufactured in the United States of America
05 04 03 02 01   10 9 8 7 6 5 4 3 2 1

PREFACE

Over his lifetime Ben Casey has "been around" so to speak, but never has he called any place home which was more than a stone's throw from where he was born. If home is truly where the heart is, Ben has and always will live within earshot of the Neuse River. We're talking about coastal North Carolina, particularly Craven and Pamlico Counties.

When Ben was a boy, Pamlico County was essentially of two classes—a handful of "haves" and everybody else. He and his family, with "Mama" as head of house, were not among the handful. Life was not easy, but the struggle provided many opportunities. Underlying the challenges of every-day life was "Mama's" moral rectitude and her ceaseless mantra—"If you want to amount to something Ben, you have to go to college." A simple admonishment, but it led Ben through a graduate degree program at Duke University.

Ben's education began long before college. His working career started at age eleven. Throughout his youth and early manhood, paying his way, his resume includes, among other things, a paper route, yard mowing, baiting commercial crab lines, harvesting tobacco, delivering milk, grocery store clerk, chicken farm labor, post office worker, health department employee, working in a bathtub factory, ad salesman, newspaper columnist, photographer and "after careers" as a ferry boat deckhand, plant nursery employee, newspaper reporter, and delivering rental cars.

Presently Ben and his wife Emmy own and operate a studio and art gallery in Oriental, North Carolina. For both fun and profit, he works a side job as a breakfast waiter at M&M's, Oriental's most famous restaurant.

What can be gleaned from such a vast array of work and educational experience?

The recording of human experience for Ben Casey, with both depth and humor, is his effort to share profound philosophical insight—into both the ordinary and the extraordinary. He calls many of these recorded observations—reality checks.

Ben Casey's reflections are more than stories about growing up. They shed light on the fact that growing up is never finished.

—*Bob Loftin*
1931-2000

FOREWORD

One could call Ben Casey a true Renaissance Man, but at only slightly more than 50 years old, he surely wasn't born in the 16th century. Some have described him as a half bubble off center.

Those who know him, know that behind his light banter and jokes, there lies a soul who appreciates life on this planet in very special ways. This book reflects a common sense...sometimes humorous...and quite philosophical reaction to life.

—Dave Feldkamp

DEDICATION

Emmy
Mary Lee
Tommy & Duncan

INTRODUCTION

Mama died on the 55th anniversary of D-Day. She was 7 years old when World War I ended.

Almost 89 and bedridden, she didn't want to die.

Mama raised me and most of the rest of us by herself. With her own set of problems, she literally drove me crazy during a good part of my life.

Then again, there was never a moment that she wouldn't have given me the shirt off her back, as we say around these parts, or the food off her plate.

Her children were her life, (other than a good plate of collards) for as long as she lived. She used welfare help to guide two of her four offspring through college and graduate school.

A lot of me could have been a lot stronger emotionally if Mama had been emotionally stronger in some ways—but I wouldn't trade places with another human being on the face of this earth.

What sensitivity I have to the wonder of this planet and to other live creatures inhabiting this planet was impacted directly by her sensitivities.

I have tried to grow from these...expressing feelings and observations...still trying to grow.

This book is not in any shape, fashion or form - my name is...I was born...I live at....Yet it does contain many personal humorous and serious incidents which have created emotional reactions, objective responses or just plain..."Why is that?" Many of these yield reality checks—depending on perspective—of the highest or lowest order.

Growing means keeping in touch with reality, while not losing sight of dreams of the ideal.

Mama's life was characterized by sometimes brutal reality checks.

She survived almost a century of reality checks and still had the hope to her dying breath that some doctor would save her.

Reality checks for her—often severe and harsh— never diminished her hope.

Richard deCharms says all of his carrier landings were good ones. He walked away from them. Consequently, I am hoping to live to walk away from reality checks, and be better for it.

—*Ben Casey*

Mama always said,

A bird don't fly too high but what it don't have to come down to get a drink of water.

ONE

ANOTHER DEAD MULE STORY

L egend has it, according to Professor Jerry Mills from the Chapel Hill branch of North Carolina's public university system, all Southern writers will at some point in a novel or non-fiction work, write about a dead mule. Since The South has always been my home, I feel compelled to write about a dead mule.

[Generally speaking, that Chapel Hill branch of the state public university system is referred to reverently by its students and graduates as THE University of North Carolina. We Dookies, associated with Duke University located seven miles away in Durham, NC, realize it to be merely another branch of the state's university system.]

As a somewhat cute but mostly nerdy little boy, I watched all the TV westerns back in the mid '50's—

Roy Rogers, Gene Autry and Hop Along Cassidy—on my neighbors' black and white televisions...I graduated to Matt Dillon in Gun Smoke, Ward Bond in Wagon Train, Clint Eastwood in Rawhide, and one of my favorites, Richard Boone starring as Paladin in Have Gun, Will Travel. It's hard to believe now but Clint Eastwood got his start as the cowpoke Roddy Yates in Rawhide.

In 1958, I moved in with my grandfather in Arapahoe, NC who had his own black & white TV. Right down the road a piece, Mr. Davis lived in the old Reel home place across from the cotton gin. Mr. Davis had a mule that roamed the back yard with the chickens, guineas and turkeys.

(Did you note how I said "Right down the road a piece...?" Nobody has ever told me just how many feet or miles down the road a piece is, but I figure that always means you can get there from here, walking if you have to.)

Now this mule was old. This mule was so old, we kids could walk up to it, not really a him or a her, and get it to walk over to the back porch by pulling on its mane. Standing on the steps of the back porch, we could climb right up on its back. Then came the ride around the ranch. Yep, that backyard full of chickens became the Wild West, wild Indians on the chase one day, bad guys wearing black hats the next day.

On those rides, each of us acted out every single cowboy we had seen on black & white television.

If cap pistols had had live ammunition, Mr. Davis wouldn't have had a chicken left after any one of those rides.

I was so cool up on that mule. I made Mr. Davis' back yard safe. Not one single chicken was scalped by a wild Indian. Not one single guinea was robbed or killed by a bad guy wearing a black hat.

God in Heaven, think how wonderful it would be if kids today could have a mule to ride. Back then, we didn't dare kill any chickens, no matter how many times we aimed at them with menacing looking toy .45's.

Kids today kill one another for a pair of sneakers.

Anyway, like I said, that mule was old. That was 40 years ago. I figure that mule is dead now.

Two

"I'm Sorry"

I'm sorry. Sometimes, saying those words is all that's necessary.

Since lawyers now multiply faster than rabbits, lawsuits clutter the courthouses of this land, crowding the courtrooms that need to be dispensing justice. There is a time to sue, and there are times not to sue. Lawyers would have us believe, especially in personal injury cases, that there is never a time not to sue.

In the fall of 1996, stopped in a line of traffic waiting for a signal light to turn green, I suddenly heard the squeal of brakes. A split second glimpse into my rear view mirror revealed what was coming at about the same time that it came, right thru the rear end of my little pick'em up truck. The impact drove me into the car ahead of me, which was driven into the car ahead of it.

You got it, stopped dead still, I was hit so hard from behind, the chain reaction saw a total of four vehicles written up in the police report. As we say in the rural South, somebody plowed into me, with the plow probably going about 45 miles per hour. The wrecker had a difficult time dislodging his car from underneath the rear end of my truck.

The guy driving the plow, or the old Buick, naturally received the citation from the men in blue. I was sore, stiff, hurting in the neck, but went on home after just a prescription for muscle relaxants and pain killers. The investigating officer had warned me that I was going to hurt for days, even though I hadn't been cut by the flying glass as my rear windshield exploded around me.

Once home, within just two or three days, the solicitations from the personal injury lawyers started arriving in the mail. I assume they got my name from the police reports. The fact that I was blameless in the accident led them on the hunt for a lawsuit. I could sue the living daylights out of the guy that hit me. One law firm actually sent a video tape, which I never watched.

(Living daylights...ever wonder what dying daylights are? All my life I've heard the expression around these parts, "I'm going to knock the living daylights out of you if you don't stop aggravating me". If somebody's fist is programed for your nose, I guess it means your lights could go out, day or night.)

There are several reasons I didn't sue the guy. His insurance company was eager to pay all medical bills, the complete repairs to my truck, and fees to rent a car during those repairs, plus a modest fee for pain and suffering. I was not fabulously compensated, but I was adequately compensated.

And you know what else. A couple of decades ago, before lawyers became more plentiful than rabbits, I plowed into a car stopped in a line of traffic. All my insurance company had to pay was for the repairs to the other car, which was a Ford Falcon. Remember those things? They were not high dollar cars.

Let's recall that saying, "There but by the grace of God go I." Well, by the grace of God, there had gone I, and I lived to tell it, having not been sued.

But you know what else? The very first words spoken to me after I stumbled out of my crumpled little truck were from the man who had hit me.

He said, "I'm sorry."

I don't know about you, but when he's sorry, and his insurance company adequately, if not fabulously, compensates me, why should lawyers entice me to add to his problems?

One other thing. This happened in my native South, in North Carolina. He was black, I am white. We shook hands after the officer finished his paperwork, and wished each other well.

THREE

CELEBRATE...

Every once in a while, some redeeming virtues shine on network television. Most intellectuals cling to the notion that only public TV offers matter stimulating for the brain. It seems that network TV does all it can to support that hypothesis, but occasionally they break down and broadcast a moment of profound depth.

One of those moments came in the show, *Touched By An Angel*. One of the stars is Della Reese, a rhythm and blues singer from the days when I was a younger child than the one I am now. Della, as an angel, was dealing with a character driven by an obsession to run up the career ladder, rather than climb it one rung at the time.

At just the right moment, Della offered a moment of sobering truth to the character blinded by a passion for material success. She admonished the character with words worth remembering long after the commercials had signaled the end of that episode.

Della Reese, singer turned actress was given this line that for me has become immortal, "Celebrate life instead of celebrating achievement."

That brings to mind the day I got my motorcycle license. Believe me, that was a day for celebration. You see, I didn't get my license to ride a motorcycle when I was an agile young teenager. No, the desire to ride came shortly after what I think may have been my 14th mid-life crisis, right after I read Zen and the Art of Motorcycle Maintenance.

Now I've never been known for macho athletic ability. Very little machinery exists that is acclimated for my level of manual dexterity. That's why Ronnie Cockrell reminded me when I announced that I wanted a motorcycle, "My mama told me that any man that would strap a gallon of gas between his legs and light a match to it was a damn fool."

Not deterred, I got a motorcycle. After months of practicing on the back roads, evading the law, I made it to Louisburg in Franklin County, NC to the examiner's office. I had heard bad things about the patience of examiners in Nash County where I lived.

God bless a patient examiner watching a middle

aged man trying to negotiate a 600 cc motorcycle around traffic cones that seemed only inches apart. He walked over to me and said, "Mr. Casey, I'm going in now to give that lady that just got here her written test. You stay out here and practice a little more and when I come back out, we'll try again."

If there is a heaven, that examiner is headed there for sure. I passed.

All the way home, the rushing breeze around my collar cooled the sweat sliding down from underneath my helmut. I didn't perspire that day, I sweated.

As long as I live, I'll remember that ride. I found myself singing over and over one line from an old rock and roll tune, "Celebrate, celebrate—dance to the music..." About the only time I didn't sing that on the 20 mile ride home was that moment a June bug hit the visor right between my eyes. Once recovered, I picked up the tune again.

Was I celebrating achievement? Well, sort of.

But I was really celebrating life. Recalling some imparted wisdom from *Zen and the Art of Motorcycle Maintenance*, one sees things when one rides in a car, looking out the window...one feels things on a motorcycle.

From the aroma of someone's burning pile of leaves in the fall to the fragrance of honeysuckle in the spring, one feels things when one rides a motorcycle.

To feel things is to celebrate life.

I do hope I never celebrate that feeling one gets from pavement rash. That's a reality check not necessarily celebrated by bikers.

FOUR

"WHICH ROAD?" MR. FROST.

You go out to eat with somebody. You're hungry, but you're not sure about what to order. The party with you on the dinner date orders one thing. You order something else after changing your mind ten times and driving the waitress up the wall with indecision.

The dinner comes.

You wish you had ordered what the other person ordered.

Why is that?

You're in your car. The radio is on. A song by The Beach Boys is on. You're sick and tired of it because you like The Embers and Carolina's version of Beach Music, not The Beach Boys. Finally, after enduring just about the whole song, you push the button for another station. On the other station, your favorite song by The Righteous Brothers is just about over, which incidentally, is any song by The Righteous Brothers.

If you had changed stations earlier, you could have heard your favorite song by The Righteous Brothers. Instead you listened to something you didn't want to listen to while you missed the opportunity to hear something you wanted to hear.

Why is that?

Robert Frost took the road less traveled and was the better for it.

You take the road less traveled and get stuck.

Why is that?

The President of the United States is paid less than a walk-on for the Chicago Bulls basketball team is paid.

Why is that?

You go through school, college and graduate school. You become a teacher. Somebody you know from high school gets a job driving a forklift in a factory. He makes more money and has better health and retirement benefits.

And as Andy Rooney would say, "Why is that?"

Here's why.

Which is worse, to be educated with relatively little intelligence or be intelligent with no education?

Dr. Arthur D. Wenger was President of Atlantic Christian College in Wilson, NC when I was a student there in that tranquil period of the late 60's. He was also President when I was on the staff there in the 70's as Director of Student Financial Aid and Assistant Director of Admissions. During my tenure on the staff, The Viet Nam War ended. Male students no longer needed to stay in college to avoid the draft.

Technical trades were an attractive alternative to a number of students considering leaving the liberal arts curriculum. More money could be made operating a backhoe in North Carolina in 1974 than in being a schoolteacher.

Dr. Wenger gave a speech to the student body I will never forget, one which I have often quoted to ears willing to listen. He made one statement relating the value of education to all human life and career choices.

Specifically to the observation that backhoe operators made more than teachers, he said, "If I wanted to be a ditch digger, I know I would rather be an educated ditch digger than an uneducated ditch digger."

That statement goes beyond the realm of education and intelligence. Dr. Wenger's observation reflected wisdom.

Dr. Arthur D. Wenger said that it was better to be an educated ditch digger than an uneducated ditch digger.

Bill Ray was a New York policeman, a truck driver and a deck hand on a shrimp boat for two decades.

Bill Ray was an educated man in all these endeavors.

Some people, without formal higher education, become educated by absorbing knowledge and translating that knowledge to wisdom.

Bill Ray, whose address used to be wherever the shrimp boat was docked, became highly educated by absorbing what there was to learn all about him, wherever he was…or for that matter…wherever he is.

Education is of value when one absorbs knowledge, no matter where the classroom might be. Bill Ray is an example of that bit of wisdom.

But for a reality check, some people, who have framed college diplomas, never really absorbed enough knowledge to make them truly educated.

The trick is to learn to absorb knowledge. Absorbing knowledge is a precursor to wisely using knowledge, which consequently can create the often elusive … wisdom.

(Bill Ray says he went to night school, so no one should expect him to know anything during the day.)

FIVE

STREAKIN'—WHAT A CHARGE!!!

We interrupt this book to bring you the story of the Dawson's Creek streaker. Names will be withheld to protect the idiotic.

Thunderstorms, aside from being able to kill you, are majestic displays of the dynamic power of nature. On the night in question, the subject in question, just prior to going to bed, chose to sit on his front porch facing the river to allow his soul to absorb the sound and light spectacle unfolding all around him. Since it was dark, since he was just before retiring, it is of some importance to note that he was relaxing with a glass of Wholeeo and Erneeo in just his Fruit of the Looms, or they could have been Hanes. Who cares?

Suddenly the wind decided to rival the sound and the fury blasting forth from the heavens. As small tree limbs could be heard crashing toward the ground, the lightning, frequent and omnipresent, revealed that the driving rain was now horizontal. Yes, the wind had picked up.

Suddenly, the subject's wife screamed. "The truck, it's moving."

Sure enough, a strong burst of wind (I think burst sounds better than gust) blowing toward the river had actually started pushing the truck backward down the drive-way, toward the road, consequently toward the river just a few feet on the other side of the road. There was no time to lay blame on whoever had driven it last leaving it out of gear with the brake off.

The subject, clad only in those little Fruit of the Looms or Hanes or whatever, momentarily forgot what the legendary physics teacher, Jimmy Smith, had taught him at New Bern High School a few decades ago. The subject thought the truck would roll a few feet and stop.

But Jimmy Smith did teach him about inertia, that property that says if the wind starts moving a truck, DOWN toward the river, that truck is going to keep on rolling DOWN toward the river until somebody runs out there in their underwear amidst the driving rain, the falling limbs and the streaks of lightning to stop it.

He hesitated. He would have never won a relay race the way he fumbled the passing of the glass of Wholeeo and Erneeo to his wife. Off he went, chasing the truck down the driveway. He managed to get inside and stop it just as it rolled out onto the road.

It's pitch dark. A thunderstorm is streaking the darkness like a scene from a Boris Karloff horror movie. This is the main road from the Minnesott Ferry to Oriental...and this truck is sitting there with the subject just realizing that Fruit of the Looms have no pockets. That he discovered when he reached for a pocket to get his keys to start the truck to get out of harm's way. No pocket, no keys.

That meant streaking back to the house, scantily clad, dodging lightning all the way.

The keys retrieved, that meant streaking back to the truck, scantily clad, dodging lightning all the way.

The incident safely concluded, dripping all over the front porch, he was so thankful that the flow of electrons in the lightning had not flown through him.

His wife said, "Oh, I am so thankful. I was afraid the truck was going to roll into the river."

That folks, is a reality check on priorities.

Six

Anticipation to Disappointment

You're riding down the road, somewhere out in the country.

Up ahead, a distinctive black column of smoke is marking the horizon. It's far enough away that it takes a couple of minutes to get near it. As the road winds and turns, you wonder if the fire is on this road or up some other road that's nearby.

Actually, you're hoping the fire will be right beside the road you're traveling. You know you will be disappointed if you get near the smoke and discover it's off in the woods, up, or down some side road. You want to see the fire that's making the smoke that's down the road that's taking more of your attention than the song playing on the radio.

You get closer. It appears the fire is on or right near the road now traveled. You speed up a little, but cautiously, expecting every next turn to reveal an array of fire trucks and ambulances all over the highway.

Speculation mounts. Is it a house, a barn, some store?

You get around that last curve that has to be just before the great source of combustion. Anticipation has reached its peak.

A man is burning a big pile of trash. There are no fire trucks. There is no danger to life or property.

You feel let down and disappointed.

Human nature— reality check #468.

SEVEN

A YARN IS NOT A LIE

There can be humor in deception, at least for the observer of the humor.

At the expense of a poor lady in Nash County whose sink may still be stopped up, the late and very legendary Rudolph Baines provided a little humor at her expense.

Rudolph worked with his brother Asbury in Peoples Hardware in Nashville, NC. This was the general store of not only hardware for Nashville, but also a number of mechanical services. Asbury's son, Marshall, and his son, Jamie, worked on everything from household lamps to chain saws, from water pumps to kerosene heaters. Marshall and Jamie were also always on call for plumbing work. That in no way meant that you could always get ahold of either one of them when you needed them.

Rudolph never took Johnny Carson's place because NBC just didn't know about him. Also, I don't think being big time on TV would have been as much fun to Rudolph as simply being Rudolph on Pleasant Grove Church Road. Rudolph, I profess, never told lies. He told yarns.

Here is an example.

Rudolph was on the phone with a lady who had obviously called several times to get Marshall or Jamie to come to her house and unstop her sink. Rudolph, always the diplomat, even if he was cussing you out, kept telling the lady that he was surprised Marshall hadn't already fixed her problem. He told her that Marshall had left to go do the job some time ago.

I remember him saying to her over the phone, "Mame, if you'll look out your front window, you'll probably see him driving up your driveway right now."

Rudolph hung up the phone — finally.

He turned to Marshall, who was standing right there the whole time, and said, "Marshall, when are you going out yonder and fix that woman's sink?"

When a man tells a lie, he's guilty of a major infraction of the rules.

A yarn, on the other hand, if your sink is not stopped up, is a little less of an infraction.

And then there was the time Rudolph's farm neighbor, Don Glisson, had cows loose all over the road in front of Rudolph's house. Rumor was that Don believed that no more fence wire had been available since World War II, so he kept making do with what he had.

Passing by there on my way to church early one Sunday, I discovered moo-mania all over the highway. I pulled into Rudolph's and woke him up. Rudolph, not necessarily in the mood to chase cows, said, "Here, use my phone and call Don, but don't tell him that you are at my house."

I would rather have a Rudolph around telling yarns making life a little lighter in a heavy world than to be around those with no such gift.

In reality, check the lies and tolerate the yarns.

MAMA ALWAYS SAID,

"A car don't run without gas; your body won't run without food in the stomach."

EIGHT

"YOU CAN GO RIGHT ON BACK."

A little bit of Harry the harried homeowner resides in all of us.

Well, almost all of us.

Some guys own every tool for everything and can fix anything. Usually these tools can easily be retrieved from their properly numbered spots on pegboard that lines the garage workshop which has a polished floor.

Go in Andy Polo's garage in Oriental, NC and you'll know what I mean. His polyurethane coated floor there is cleaner and shinier than most dinner plates.

The late Erma Bombeck had one word of advice for people living next door to the Andy Polo's of the world. These are the people whose cars are always washed and waxed, the driveway perfectly edged, the yard seeded and fertilized, manicured better than the Augusta Country Club just prior to The Masters.

Irma says if you live next door to somebody like that and you want to stay sane, "Move."

On a good day, one might be able to see some of the floor in my workshop. When I walk through either the doors of The Village Hardware in Oriental, NC or Pamlico Home Builders in Bayboro, NC, the clerks get together for a big laugh as to who gets picked to entertain questions about the latest mechanical failure at my home.

Once, to save money, I rented a power washer from the late and legendary Ray Creech at Neuse Builders in Oriental to scour down the house prior to the big paint job—which I must add, I did complete myself.

I asked, "Ray, can people with limited intelligence and limited abilities operate that power washer?"

Ray stared at me through a long pause.

Finally he replied, "Yeah, you can."

I asked that question in a generic way. Note, Ray was specific in his response.

I get it home and with thousands of pounds of pressure I blast away mold and mildew from the front and one end of my house. I drag it around back.

Around back, I discover I have stretched the hose so much I have broken the coupling connecting the water supply line to the pressure pump. Give me credit. I instantly remembered Ray's words of caution, "Don't dare run the pump without water running to it or the pump will burn up."

I made a lightening leap to shut off the engine...only I tripped over a hose, fell and stretched out my hand to break my fall...said hand landing right on the muffler atop that Briggs & Stratton engine.

On that muffler, my hand supported the whole weight of my body.

Need I say more? Mufflers are hot, very hot.

Jumping ahead, caring wife, Emmy, is rushing me to Pamlico Medical Center in Bayboro. She drives as I hold my hand in a casserole dish of ice water sitting in my lap. She rounds sharp curves as fast as was prudent, but even with that prudence the ice water sloshed over the sides and chilled my lap.

Chilling my lap was no problem. But what about the wet pants...you know where.

I bound into the lobby at Pamlico Medical Center holding a casserole dish with one hand that's holding my other hand.

Betty, the receptionist, took one long look at me

from head to toe and said, "You can go on back."

In reality, that's a way to get ushered right back to an examining room if you can check the stares and the laughs.

NINE

YOUR BRAIN—KEEP IT WITH YOU

There are some things one should not leave home without.

The brain is one of those commodities best never left behind. I've left my brain behind too many times...and too many times have been left behind.

In 1996, just a few weeks after moving to this garden spot of the world in Eastern North Carolina where the real Dawson's Creek empties into the Neuse River not far from where it empties into the Pamlico Sound, Hurricane Fran paid a visit to my humble little abode on this sliver of land separating the river from the creek.

The morning of her impending arrival brought the initial gusty winds and rain showers. My very great, but sadly my late neighbor, Bruce Godfrey and I decided we had waited long enough to retrieve our small little outboards from the creek. It was time to bring them on shore and secure them under our carports.

This involved driving the boats to the boat ramp about a mile from the house, then loading them on trailers to be pulled home.

He drove his truck with trailer in tow to the ramp. I followed him in my little truck. We left his truck and trailer there and drove back home in my truck. The next task was to drive his boat to the ramp.

His boat wouldn't start. No problem. I could give him a tow with my boat. By now, the showers are a steady downpour, the winds are a sustained ominous sign of what's going to come that afternoon and night.

I drive my boat down to his dock. My little boat is steered by the tiller handle on the motor, which also serves as the throttle. If you know boats, you know what I am describing. If you don't know boats, well, this is a basic little boat that you steer, not with a steering wheel, but by turning the motor, using the motor as a rudder.

Got the picture?

Bruce tosses me a rope. (Boat people call all ropes lines. Foxhunters don't hunt with dogs, but with hounds. Aren't you impressed?) I grab it and notice that there is no convenient place to tie it on the stern of my boat. No problem. I'll just hold onto the rope with my left hand while I steer and drive my little vessel with my right hand. I twist the right hand, which revs the throttle. The slack is taken up in the towrope...and...you guessed it...my left arm is almost pulled out of its socket, almost pulling me overboard.

That was the first sign that a brain had been left behind.

Recovering, with the rain pelting away at us, I manage to hold onto the towrope and slowly get us to the boat ramp. Once there, we awkwardly maneuver his boat to the little pier alongside the ramp. I back away about the same time a gust of wind reminds us why we are doing this. I react by twisting that right hand.

Remember my right hand? It activates the throttle. Twisting that hand in one direction revs up the throttle, the other direction, slows the motor down. Remember Murphy's Law? Guess which way I twisted the right hand.

Anyway, I didn't back too far into the reeds and marsh grass before letting go of the throttle.

One more sign the brain had been left at home.

After only three tries, Bruce managed to get his trailer backed down the ramp and we load his boat for a routine ride home. We park it in his yard and return to my house, get in my truck for the return trip to the ramp to get my boat.

The ladies of the two households have decided to wait out this project on my front porch. They watch us leave in the now almost horizontal rain ...that means the wind has picked up if you don't know about horizontal rain...and Bruce's wife turns to my wife and asks, "Where are they going?"

My wife says, "Well, they're going to get our boat now."

Bruce's wife then asks, "Well why don't they have your trailer hooked up to your truck?"

Bruce and I had made it to the turn off from the paved road onto the gravel road leading to the ramp when we discovered we were traveling sans trailer. Traveling back home, we knew we were going to be in for some hard inquiries from the wives.

We decided the best way to describe that third sign of brains being left at home was to say that the trip without the trailer in my truck was merely a reconnaissance run.

They knew better.

But there are others who have left home without a full complement of brains. It happened to a complement of volunteer firemen. The township will not be named in order to protect the guilty.

A fire broke out in the vicinity of the homes of a

goodly number of volunteer firemen. This goodly number of volunteer firemen jumped into their pick-ups and various and sundry other vehicles to converge on the site of the errant combustion at about the same time.

They emerged from their vehicles at about the same time, looked at one another until one of them said, "Somebody better go to the station and get a fire truck."

Folks, that's really a reality check.

All kinds of people have been known to leave home, sans brains.

I have done it. And sometimes my writing is like that of a reporter who worked for a daily paper in a North Carolina town. The managing editor of that paper said, "He sits down, puts the typewriter in gear and his brain in neutral."

That reporter wasn't me, but it could have been.

Leaving the brain behind does not leave one without an ultimate destination.

TEN

SAUCE CAN BE ART...
ART CAN BE SAUCE

L et's talk about art and barbecue sauce.

First of all, we can easily define both of these entities. Actually, art is a lot easier to define than barbecue. Art is the process of creative expression by individuals, singularly or collectively. Paintings, sculptures, etc, and so forth and so on are the products of art, but for the sake of expediency, are often called art.

In one sense, art is more like a verb in that it is this active process of creative expression, but the word process is itself a noun.

There is a similar dichotomy with barbecue. In

the real world, ie, my part of North Carolina, barbecue is 99.987% a noun. Barbecue is the meat from a pig that has been slow-roasted, preferably over live coals, and seasoned with a sauce made of vinegar, crushed red pepper, butter, salt and in some cases a hint of brown sugar, but nothing whatsoever that is a derivative from a tomato.

A lot of people question whether or not various consequences of creative expression are really art, just as some people question whether or not tomato based barbecue sauces are really barbecue sauces.

I can answer the question once and for all right now.

First of all, the product of any creative expression is art. A small child scrawling on a piece of paper with a crayon is producing art. A hoodlum painting a wall with a spray can is producing art.

That art may not be sophisticated art, it may not be good art, but it's art. If it's the product of creative expression, it is art. The judgment about sophistication or quality is a matter not to be undertaken at this point.

Yes, that means even those tacky pink flamingos flocked together along driveways in some subdivisions represent creative expression. Yes, that means the homeowner owns art...might be tacky art in the eyes of some sophisticates, but it's art.

Remember, we're not discussing the different kinds of art, we're simply setting the record straight as to what is art.

While any form of creative expression is art, not any barbecue sauce is barbecue sauce. Any barbecue sauce with anything in it that is derived from a tomato is not a barbecue sauce, it's an aberration.

Also, slow roasted beef seasoned with any kind of sauce is not barbecue. Barbecue, as I pointed out earlier, is dead pig, slow-cooked and seasoned with vinegar, red pepper, butter, possibly a little sugar and salt.

In some parts of the country, people cook beef and call it barbecue. They are wrong. There, I've set them straight. One caveat, barbecue is an adjective when describing chicken that has been slow cooked and seasoned with barbecue sauce, i.e., barbecue chicken.

Also, in some parts of the country, people often refer to cooking out on a grill as barbecuing. They say things like, "Let's barbecue a steak tonight." That sentence is full of oxymorons. You grill a steak, something that cannot become barbecue because steak comes from dead cows, not dead pigs.

I am happy to provide this insight for the nation and the world and to set the record straight in a definitive way as to what is art and what is barbecue sauce, as to what is barbecue and what is not barbecue.

Are there any questions?

For those with questions, this is reality check # 642.

ELEVEN

WHEN A LITTLE TOWN IS REALLY BIG

Had Norman Rockwell been there, the scene would have definitely appeared on the cover of the next issue of The Saturday Evening Post. I was cruising east toward the capital of Pamlico County on Intrastate 55.

Stonewall is just east of Bayboro. I had made it through Stonewall's suburbs and was rounding the curve that makes up the major intersection in the central part of the downtown section.

We're talking about the only intersection in downtown Stonewall. Suddenly, silhouetted against the sky before me was a giant John Deere combine parked in my lane of traffic.

It is not too uncommon to see combines on the road in late fall.

But it is quite uncommon to see a combine parked with a stepladder perched atop the grain storage section of the combine. Likewise, it is uncommon to see two men holding the stepladder while a third is perched on the top steps hanging Christmas decorations from light pole to light pole.

A vast number of similar municipalities would have employed a boom truck with a bucket to lift workmen to the heights necessary to adorn the downtown streets with a "Season's Greeting." Assuming that Stonewall does not itself own a boom truck, it is only logical to assume that town fathers (and to be politically correct, I guess I should throw in the town mothers as well) chose the frugal option of borrowing Charles Alexander's combine to do the job.

Jimmy Spain was directing traffic around this holiday endeavor. He informed me that the mayor of Stonewall was up on the ladder because he was not imminently qualified to direct traffic on the street level. I am not sure if Stonewall has a mayor, but anyway that's what Jimmy Spain told me.

I don't hesitate to say that seeing grown men on a Sunday afternoon park a combine in the middle of the street as a perch from which to hang Christmas decorations makes me feel mighty good about my fellow man.

Intrastate 55 through downtown Stonewall may not be Fifth Avenue in New York. It may not be the site of Macy's Christmas parade. No, it's not these...it's a whole hell of a lot better.

And when it comes to small town America, which for me is small town Pamlico County, let me also share with you an experience my friend Hawkeye had last week. Hawkeye, who lives in Oriental, has been so nicknamed because he has the reputation of being able to inventory a yard sale while riding by at 45 miles per hour.

Hawkeye passed a couple walking. Using his "hawkeye" instinct, he figured this couple to be just off a boat, probably from one of the many sailboats making the voyage South this time of year on the intra-coastal waterway.

He stopped to exchange pleasantries. Sure enough, the couple had been in town for a week while repairs were being made to their vessel at a local boatyard.

After offering them any assistance to make their stay enjoyable, Hawkeye was confronted with a question from the traveling duo. They asked, "Sir, is there an ordinance in this town that requires every-body to wave to everyone they pass on the street?"

Hawkeye advised them that everyone waved to everyone. He explained that it was better to wave to everyone than to fail to recognize even the most casual of acquaintances and fail to offer a greeting. Such a "high-hatting" is virtually unforgivable in small-town America, especially small-town Pamlico County.

[Y'all know what "high-hatting" is? It is snubbing somebody because you think you are richer or better than them. It's something ten-cent millionaires do all the time to people they think beneath them.

Oh. Y'all know what ten-cent millionaires are? It's those people who think they are rich, act rich—but wind up borrowing a dime for a cup of coffee—back when a cup of coffee was only a dime. Now, I guess they would be called just one-dollar millionaires, considering inflation.]

All of this falls in line with this week's words of wisdom from the noted 20th century philosopher, Dave Shirk. Shirk shared with me this guide for life, "He who is wrapped up in himself makes a very small package."

People who stand on a ladder perched atop a John Deere combine to hang a town's Christmas decorations...people who wave to all they meet...these are people who make a mighty big package of humanity, in Pamlico County, North Carolina...and the world.

MAMA ALWAYS SAID,

(when referring to drunk or obstinate people)
"You can't argue with a sign post."

The phrase "small town America," is often the stimulus for thoughts of tranquility and pastoral scenes that adorn calendars and greeting cards. Hallmark and American Greetings don't usually decorate Christmas cards with "big town America," pictures of skyscrapers, interstate highways or steel mills.

Quantity does not make for quality. The people of Lowland, on the lower end of Pamlico County, NC, understand that.

There is only one road leading to Lowland. Get to the end of it, you either turn around and leave the same way you came or you leave by boat.

But leave Lowland on that narrow two-lane road and a drive of only three hours will put one in the midst of world class universities, medical centers, a major multi-national research center, museums, galleries, a state symphony and an international airport.

For people of Lowland, that three-hour drive is a small price to pay to be able to cling to small town America.

A scary thought. What if too many people in big town America realize what they're missing by not living in small town America? What if they start moving to small town America?

What if suddenly there should be no more small town America? God forbid that from happening to Lowland!

TWELVE

MONKEYS MAY NOT BE UNCLES BUT THEY ARE SMART NEIGHBORS

Where do you stand in the fight of evolution over creation...or creation over evolution?

Why aren't evolution and creation one and the same thing?

Who is ashamed to be part of the same developing chain that developed monkeys?

I submit to you that monkeys are ashamed to be part of the same process that created human beings?

Would monkeys destroy their habitat with reckless abandon the way man has destroyed his habitat?

Would a monkey jump out of a tall tree onto a big

rock below because he didn't get invited to some big banana dance by fellow monkeys?

In other words, are monkeys dumb enough to commit suicide?

Darwin was perhaps more right than we know with his premise about the survival of the fittest. If you look at monkeys, they might feel themselves to be a hell of a lot more fit than we humans running to psychiatrists and analysts every week taking mind altering drugs to help us cope with the jungle that we have created ourselves.

Monkeys do fairly well with what was the natural, unaltered jungle that the great Creator created.

Man has a harder time living with the alterations he has made to this planet.

Thirteen

Not All Shining Trucks Are Polished

I nequity is often the trademark of American society.

Don't believe me? Why do we polish firetrucks but seldom wash garbage trucks?

Why do we virtually deify fire trucks and firemen while taking for granted the men who daily toil in every climatic condition imaginable to save our homes from destruction?

Yes, garbage men toil every day to save our homes from destruction. Don't believe me? Try living with your garbage?

Fire doesn't take as long to kill you or destroy your possessions, but disease, pestilence and rodents from the pile up of garbage are just as deadly and destructive.

Let's paint garbage trucks fire engine red, or for better visibility in a variety of weather conditions, let's go with the nouveau lemon yellow. Let's put a mixture of red and strobe lights all over the top of the packers. Let's add a siren to sound every time the truck moves from one house to the next.

Let's start having bake sales and sell barbecue plates to raise money to buy protective clothing and new equipment for the men who answer the call to haul away our trash.

Let's establish a Sanitation Department Ladies Auxiliary. Let's start having Garbagemen's Day in rural communities just like the old fashioned Firemen's Day.

Let's establish a Garbageman's Museum on parity with the New Bern Fireman's Museum in every town.

In no way whatsoever am I taking cheap shots at firemen whom I respect and appreciate.

But let's give respect to all who deserve it.

In reality, a child may not ever get as excited to see a garbage truck as he is a fire truck, but he should be just as thankful.

FOURTEEN

"ACTING" THE ROLE OF HERO

Friends, Romans and countrymen, I come to bury John Wayne's acting, not to praise it.

The late Duke was loyal to the nation that had afforded him great celebrity status. All that said in his honor and memory, I do have a problem with labeling him as a great actor.

Compare John Wayne to Dustin Hoffman.

John Wayne could play John Wayne better than anybody, but John Wayne is all John Wayne could play.

Dustin Hoffman, from Little Big Man to Midnight Cowboy to All The President's Men to Tootsie, can play any role or character. That's true acting.

Could you picture John Wayne as Tootsie?

I just felt like expressing this for a reality check on what is really the art of being a dramatic actor or actress.

Before I get crucified by fans of the Duke, let me say I really like John Wayne playing John Wayne. But I admire the ability of Dustin Hoffman to play any character you ask him to play.

Playing the role of a hero doesn't necessarily make one a hero.

MAMA ALWAYS SAID,

"Cake's always better the next day, after the flavor has gone through it."

Albert Speight was a hero.

He worked cleaning eggs for Wyatt Taylor when he was three quarters of a century old, long after most men had retired. He lived almost two miles from the poultry farm. Consequently, Mr. Wyatt, as he was affectionately called, always gave Albert a ride to and from work.

One Saturday, Mr. Wyatt was injured in an automobile accident. Word traveled fast through the Greene County, NC countryside. Albert Speight heard of his employer's misfortune. He knew somebody had to go to the chicken houses that afternoon to gather eggs and tend to the feeding.

Without saying anything to anyone, Albert walked nearly two miles, did the necessary chores, and walked home, never hinting for praise, honor or monetary reward.

Albert Speight was never played by John Wayne on the big screen. But Albert Speight was a real hero.

FIFTEEN

... MY GIRL, MY GIRL ...

I was riding down the road listening to the radio. It being the Christmas season, there appeared on the speakers the familiar carol, The First Noel.

[By the way, when someone is riding, on a car, not in it, why are they always riding down the road instead of up the road? Up or down, terminology in the South—"I'll pick you up on my car," translates to—"I'll stop for you and give you a ride in my car."]

I found myself singing along, visualizing myself before a cathedral size audience, standing before a microphone, singing the lines a capella. There wasn't an eye or an ear in the whole place that wasn't tuned into me.

Can I sing? Lee Marvin sang in Paint Your Wagon.

Johnny Cash gets a lot of money and adulation from people.

I've sung My Girl in the shower more times than The Temptations have performed it on stage.

But then there was Peggy Roberts. Peggy stood beside me for awhile as we seventh and eighth graders practiced the Christmas concert at Arapahoe Elementary School in 1959.

This was back in the days when anybody would have been tarred and feathered who would have challenged the right of the local elementary school to sing religious Christmas carols in a school production.

There were some things that were good about the good old days.

At any rate, Peggy Roberts asked Mrs. Perry, the music teacher, to move her because she just couldn't sing beside Benjie Casey.

I sang My Girl, alone, in the shower, not on stage.

I sang The First Noel. in the car, alone, not in a packed cathedral.

What would we be without our fantasies?

For voices like mine, fantasy is reality.

Those who stand in the shower crooning, "My girl, my girl…,"
living in a fantasy world of bright lights and microphones, surely
would be groomed at the Playboy Barber Shop before every performance.

Sixteen

Why does less cost more?

Have you ever bought Breyer's All Natural Vanilla ice cream? I'm sure you have.

Did you check the ingredients? There are only four commodities that make up Breyer's vanilla ice cream...milk, cream, pure sugar and natural vanilla.

Those four ingredients make for some pretty darn good ice cream. I recently brought home a half gallon of the stuff for $3.99. In the good old days, when I was a bag boy and checker for the A&P in the Five Points area of New Bern, a half gallon of Marvel ice cream would often be on sale for forty-nine cents.

Times don't change, but prices surely do.

New Bern was and still is proud to be home to Maola Milk & Ice Cream Company. My fourth grade teacher, Mrs. Duffy took us there for a field trip. Field trips there now include a stop at the Cow Cafe for the best hot dogs in town as well as more different flavors of ice cream than one could ever sample in a lifetime.

I recently purchased a half-gallon of Maola's cherry vanilla ice cream for $3.09, ninety cents less than Breyer's.

Now remember, Breyer's vanilla has only four ingredients.

Guess how many different things are put in a gallon of Maola cherry vanilla for ninety cents less...seventeen.

Is there something wrong with this picture?

Maola cherry vanilla ice cream includes skim milk, cream, sugar, corn syrup, cherries, high fructose corn syrup, whey, guar gum, mono & diglycerides, annatto, natural flavors, cellulose gum, polysorbate 80, Red 3, citric acid, carrageenan and locust bean gum.

First thing that comes to mind...what is a guar ...is it an animal or some kind of plant or tree? How do you get gum from a guar? Why do you need gum from a guar in ice cream?

And cellulose gum. Isn't cellulose fiber a tree product? What's a carrageenan? Is polysorbate 80 better than polysorbate followed by some other number like 70 or 90?

Let's talk about labor.

Doesn't it take a tremendous more amount of labor to mix 17 ingredients than it does four? Think of just the purchasing and inventorying of ingredients. Why is an ice cream with 17 ingredients 22.556390977% less in retail cost than an ice cream with only four ingredients?

I won't address the issue of taste here.

It would seem to me that either Breyer's is way over-charging or Maola officials have been out to lunch for too long a time? It almost makes me think Maola may be like the guy who bought a load of watermelons for $1.00 each, had such success selling them for $1.00 each, that he went back and bought another load to sell the same way.

This is a serious question. How is it possible for a company to procure, inventory and blend together in their product, seventeen different ingredients and sell it for 22.556390977% less than what another company using only four ingredients charges?

Let me ask you one more time...is there something wrong with this picture?

Who's due for a reality check here, Maola, Breyer's or those of us who think a bowl of ice cream cures all aches and pains?

MAMA ALWAYS SAID,

"Breakfast is your most important meal."

Seventeen

And The Bonus Is ...

My greatest possession, other than being loved, is where I live. I live on one acre of sand that is bounded by creek and river.

Some watch the sun rise or set on a land-bound horizon. I watch it with double vision, seeing it in the sky, and simultaneously in the water's surface.

This is a double blessing...a multiple blessing. Ducks dive beneath the surface for food, pelicans sail effortlessly just inches above the water, seagulls bomb the surface in that never-ending quest that makes up an ecological cycle; and great blue herons punctuate the stillness with great squawking concertos.

Out in a boat with Ken O'Neill, trying to catch

fish, but more realistically soaking bait, rocked by gentle waves lapping against the side of the boat, soaking all of this in, into the fabric of our shirts and shorts stained with the aroma of bait shrimp—and our memory banks—Ken observes, "Out here, catching a fish is just a bonus."

Is that not a reality check of the highest order?

It is also a link to both the spiritual and physical beauty of this world. It links us with a purpose for being granted the opportunity to be on this planet.

It is the link to all hopes for today...and...whatever tomorrows might come our way.

MAMA ALWAYS SAID,

(referring to either misbehavior or disrespect)
"It'll come home to you
when you have children of your own."

From Hemingway's story of the old man and the sea to Ken O'Neil's observation that catching fish is merely a bonus while passing quiet time on the water, fishing has captivated man's imagination for millennium after millennium.

Give a man a fish, feed him one meal. Teach a man to fish, feed him for a lifetime.

Billie Truitt learned how to fish as a boy and has fed and clothed his family for a lifetime by harvesting the sea. Fishing has been more than a way of life for him, it has been his life.

Summer's heat and winter's frigid winds have joined forces to carve deep lines in Billie Truitt's face. Explore those crevices and you will find the beauty of simplicity, a life not complicated by dot.com, the stock market or any kind of personal identity crisis.

Called for jury duty once, Billie Truitt responded to the judge's question about his ability to serve—not with "Your Honor..."—but with, "Well, Capt'n, I get up early every morning to go fishing and by the time I get to this courtroom, I ain't going to be able to stay awake because I'll be all tired out."

Fishermen are known to address everyone as "Capt'n," even those frequently called "Your Honor".

The judge simply said to Billie, "You're excused".

That was a simple answer to a man living a life of simplicity as a fisherman...in this case, a true waterman.

Eighteen

Mirror Of My Soul

Hank Thoreau cranked out more than a few words about Walden Pond. In infinite detail, he described the pond and the local environment there from season to season.

I have a Walden Pond. It's Dawson's Creek and the Neuse River.

I've heard that a man who grew up in either the mountains or by the water and subsequently moved away, was never happy until he returned. I am living proof of that premise.

I grew up with the Trent and Neuse Rivers in New Bern as my back yard. I learned to swim in the Neuse River. When I was 11, I moved in with my grandfather, just a few miles downriver, near

Dawson's Creek. I became somewhat of a man the day I was brave enough to jump off the old Dawson's Creek bridge into the deep water where the creek flows into the river.

Notice I tell about jumping from the bridge. One of my teenage idols was Jack Broughton. Jack was Carolyn's older brother. Jack played football. Nobody messed with Jack. Jack dived off the bridge. He didn't jump feet-first like I did.

And Carolyn, Jack's sister. What's there to tell about falling in love in the sixth grade?

At any rate, I moved away from these rivers when I went away to college. I stayed away for 31 years. Thank God...yes, I thank God in heaven that I have been granted the opportunity to return to my Walden Pond.

What is it about the river that flows in a man's soul?

Does the river portray a man's soul when its surface is still and white like glass, calm with no visible movement?

- when its surface is deep blue, with gentle ripples?
- when it is silver gray in the middle of windless days?
- when its color reflects the fleeting changes in the skies?
- when it looks more brown than blue or gray?

- when it is broken with white caps, a strong wind whipping the surface into a pattern of constant motion?

- when a hurricane or nor'easter violently thrashes the waves upon the shoreline?

- when rain and fog create a wall of white?

- when it is dotted with boats putting out nets, men working on the eternal harvest from the sea, much the same way Peter did in the time of Christ, only this time with an engine on the boat?

- when pelicans skim the surface before snatching a fish away?

- when seagulls soar overhead before dive-bombing to the surface to snatch a fish away?

- when diving ducks sit patiently on the surface before disappearing for what seems an eternity into the brink to snatch a fish?

- when the rising sun paints the surface with orange, then a white-hot white?

- when the setting sun paints the surface with every imaginable orange, pink, purple and magenta?

- on calm nights when reflections of bright stars are mirrored on its surface?

- when the lights of homes on the other side are bounced on top of the waves?

- when thunderclouds shape the color and design of the surface of the water in patches and patterns that match the sky?

- when it is the stage for a ballet performed by bottle-nosed porpoises, our dolphins?

* because its ever-changing nature is something that will never change?

To all of the above, yes.

My Neuse River, my Dawson's Creek—my Walden Pond...portrays my soul.

Shorelines are forever changing.

Scattered along the shores of the Neuse River, as well as many other waterways all across America, are the remains of man's futile attempts to protect and preserve man's interest in the shore-lines.

The remnants of my neighbor's bulkhead of wood and stone on the river's shores testify to the power of the water to shift not only the sands, but man's barricades intended to prevent that shifting.

While the sands of the shoreline are forever shifting, my soul's home will forever follow that shift.

NINETEEN

DOES THIS MAKE SENSE?

Is it possible to observe a phenomenon in nature and draw a conclusion that makes sense, but, relatively speaking, makes no sense?

My house is a few miles from the Cherry Point Marine air base. We civilians often just say Cherry Point or the air base. Those military types always refer to it as MCAS Cherry Point, for Marine Corps Air Station Cherry Point.

Military types are not often known for an economy of words like famous writers. Who was it who said, "Why use two words when only one will do?"

But that's way off the subject at hand.

A straight line can be drawn from my house to one of the main runways at MCAS Cherry Point, five or six miles away. I need no weatherman to tell me the direction of the wind. The sounds of freedom from overhead are all I need to tell me the wind is from the southwest.

[That means when there's a southwest wind blowing, my rooftop is an outer marker for the approach to one particular runway.]

One day I was only a couple of rungs up on a ladder while painting my storage building. Overhead, a monstrously large C-5A cargo plane was lumbering in at slow speed for a landing. The gear was down and the plane seemed to be close enough to see inside the cockpit .. although that would be an exaggeration.

I called Emmy, "Look at that, that's the lowest I've ever seen one of those things come over."

She said, "Oh, it's not any lower. You're just standing on a ladder."

It makes sense...and yet it doesn't make sense.

That's the way life is. It makes sense...and yet it doesn't make sense.

That's the reality of life.

TWENTY

GOOD EVERY DAY OF THE WEEK

I crept out of bed early this morning. It's Good Friday, 1997.

The sun hasn't risen yet, but dawn light is slithering over the creek behind our house and on the river in front of the house.

This is undoubtedly, to me anyway, the garden spot of the world. Some might argue with that assertion on those days that hurricanes choose to come ashore here. But I still stick to my claim. The morning after Hurricane Fran, the worst blow in forty years according to the lifers along this stretch of the river, my late but very great neighbor, Bruce Godfrey, surveyed what looked like a battle zone all around our homes. His profound observation was,

"Small price to pay to get to live in paradise."

The waters are flat this morning. That's rarely the case, for a little wind creates rolling swells on a river as wide as the Neuse only a few miles from where it joins the Pamlico River to form the Pamlico Sound. The Pamlico Sound is bounded by the Outer Banks, that barrier reef of islands with inlets at Cape Hatteras, Cape Lookout and Beaufort in our neck of the Sound.

It's so flat this morning that it virtually is a mirror, reflecting the gulls, a passing flock of geese and puffy clouds. I know that writers like to use things like "the water is like a mirror, reflecting...," but that's exactly the way it is this morning.

This is a good day. I just feel it. But why is it called Good Friday? In the half century that I have lived on this planet, I never have asked a preacher or a teacher why the day of a crucifixion is referred to as Good Friday. It's one of those things I have always felt like I ought to know, but don't.

How often do we fail to ask "why" or "what" when we think we are supposed to know? Ignorance can help perpetuate ignorance.

At any rate, I think this is a good day to live. I somehow can't picture myself as the stoic Indian on some old TV western of by-gone days proclaiming before going up onto a mountain, "This is a good day to die." Perhaps when the parts inside me get a little more worn out than they are now, I might come upon a good day to die. But until then, it's a good day to live.

But getting up early, watching the light unfold the beauty around me, listening to the gulls discuss the breakfast menu of menhaden and pinfish, I bet they're thinking, "It's a good day to live."

My friend Bob Inskeep, Presbyterian minister extra-ordinaire and radio personality personified, was visiting me one day at my former home in Nash County. My house was situated in the corner of a five-acre pasture. We were sitting on the front porch, as all good Southern people do when they have company during the more temperate times of the year.

[I should have asked Bob why Good Friday is called Good Friday. Why didn't I think of that?]

Bob noticed a group of dogs playing in the grass about a hundred yards or so from the house. Out of the blue he turned to me and remarked, "You know, before I drive back to Raleigh, I think I'll go down there and wallow around some with those dogs. Look at how much fun they are having playing together."

Bob and I had been discussing some of the great hardships of life...divorce, career burnout, how to care for an aging parent...the things that make us say, "Life is hard."

Life can be hard for dogs, too. But they take time to play.

It's Good Friday. It is a good Friday. It is a good day to live. It is a good day to play.

In reality, all of the above make this a good day to be thankful.

TWENTY-ONE

THANK GOD I'M A COUNTRY BOY

Sunday morning, all was quiet, not a creature was stirring, not even a mosquito.

I slipped out of bed, having been awake for some time pondering the great mysteries of life, to head out into the silver-gray dawn on the river. I was hoping to see dolphins so I could discuss great mysteries of life with them. I have been wanting to get a picture of them as they have journeyed into the Neuse from the Pamlico Sound to feast on crabs and fish. To guarantee that I would see them on this almost colorless morning, I left the camera at home.

You got it! Just as I was clearing the channel of Dawson's Creek, the water broke with that scene choreographed better than anything Baryshnikov has ever seen or done. When dolphins break the water in unison, it's more unison than any unison ever unified at Radio City Music Hall by The Rockettes.

Oh, how I wish I were a poet. Poetry describes great experiences of life with feeling. One doesn't just see dolphins in a natural ballet on the river. One feels the excitement, eagerly anticipating just where they will emerge again. Keep in mind, these aren't dolphins putting on a rehearsed show at some tourist attraction in Florida. This is real life on the high seas, or the high river.

I followed them from Dawson's Creek, past Camp Don Lee, past Camp Sea Gull, all the way to the ferry terminal at Minnesott. I would lose sight of them and would frantically search the horizon for their repeated performance of grand entrees. Never disappointed, they often surfaced right beside me, no more than 10 or 12 feet away.

I wanted to jump overboard and swim with them. I wanted to pet them, to rub them, to see them smile with their bottlenose faces. I wanted to...but I sometimes am aware of my limits.

This is the summer. Entertainment news is filled with predictions and reports about blockbuster movies and box office receipts. Give me a break! Hollywood can never and will never, no matter how much computers can generate special effects, match the spectacle one finds in the natural world. Theme parks and rock concerts attract the young. What happened to an age when miracles in the wilds captivated the imaginations of, as Ringling Brothers would put it, "children of all ages?"

I've been around right at a half a century. Thank God I'm a country boy, (thanks to John Denver), and thank God I'm still a boy, still a child.

Though still a child, I did heed the wisdom of adults and did not pursue the dolphins across the wake of the ferryboat just pulling out from Minnesott. There are limits to little boats with little outboard engines.

Turning around, I headed back east, down river. By then, the sun was that summertime hazy, reddish-orange ball glowing through the haze of a July dawn. I steered the boat right into the reflection of that solar miracle on the slick surface of the gently rolling swells in the river.

I wasn't blinded by the sun.

I was blinded by the feeling.

And that was reality at its best.

TWENTY-TWO

WHEN WEATHER COUNTS MOST

I've reached the check-the-obituary-page age.

When I lived in Nash County from 1975 through 1996, my excuse was to see if anybody I had known or anybody who might have at one time claimed kin to me had died back home in either New Bern or Pamlico County. Now that I'm back home in Pamlico County, I check to see if anybody I know has gone on to their reward back in Nash County.

All of that means that I've reached the age to wonder what my name will look like printed there, and more specifically, what my age might be at the anointed hour.

First of all, about my comment, "...gone on to

their reward."

As much as I try to follow the dictates of the Christian religion and all it says about Heaven, I do have my own perception about the demise of physical life here. For one thing, if we're having a good life here, and our folks are still dependent on us to do whatever it is we do around the house, then I suppose nobody considers it a reward to die.

We just simply say that stuff about going on to the great reward because it sounds like the right thing to say if there's doubt about where the departed has really gone.

Debating the if, where, or what of Heaven is not what's on my mind right now.

I just read The Sun Journal, fish wrapper for New Bern, NC. Naturally I checked the obits. Now here's what I read about the tradition known as "The Wake."

[But before I do that, y'all do know what a fishwrapper is, don't you? If you have never been to a fish market that took dressed fish, wrapped them first in butcher paper and then several layers of old newspaper, then fish markets where you grew up are not like fish markets where I grew up. Newspaper is excellent insulation to keep fish cold till it hits the pan.

And one other thing, ever wonder why they call a fish that's been decapitated and stripped of its innards—a dressed fish?]

In one death notice—don't you just like the way some papers call it the Death Notices, as opposed to the obituary page...as if somebody got a notice that they had died—the obit stated that the family would receive family and friends at the funeral home from 7-9 pm on Tuesday. Receiving family and friends for a visitation is, I guess, pretty acceptable.

But then came the goodies.

One death notice reported that "Viewing" would be from 7-9 pm on Tuesday.

As a little boy who grew up in The South, I have been to a lot of funerals that were just as much 'viewings" as they were last rites. One view of funerals in The South is the great observation of who and how many people will be there. You could semi-judge someone's worth to the community by whether or not you could see the end of the long line of cars with their headlights on if you were about half way down from the hearse in the procession to the cemetery from the church.

And speaking of who goes to funerals other than those truly paying respect, it's those who want to do that kind of viewing plus a great preponderance of local politicians should death occur within 18 months of the next election. You can always spot these two groups.

Those paying respects hug the family members and usually move on. The politicians shake hands with, instead of hug the family members, because they really don't know them that well, Then they proceed to shake hands with every other soul there with that all familiar greeting, "Jack, or John or Doe or whomever, it's so good to see you...so good to see you...so good to see you ..., " and on and on and on.

But what I really want to get to is the real "viewers," those who come to view "the body." Note that I said "the body," I didn't refer to the departed as having a name. For some reason, once you die, you are no longer Jack or Jill or whoever, you are "the body."

Here are samples from my 5 decades of funeral going.

"Oh, she looks so peaceful."—I can live with that. Death does bring a final peace.

Then there's "Looks just like him."—Gimme a break. Show me somebody who went around in life looking like somebody laid out in a coffin and I'll show you somebody that was not a well person while they were alive.

"Oh, she's looks so pretty. That dress looks so good on her. Pink was her color."

"Mmmm, he looks so good in that coat and tie. You know he never did wear one."

"You reckon they really are going to bury her that ring on?"

"Well they did a good job. I never expected him to look that good."

"Well, I don't know, I don't think his mouth looks right."

"Did they have to do an autopsy? You know they never look right if they do that."

So help me, as Dave Barry, humor columnist for the Miami Herald would say, "I am not making this up." I have actually heard these comments from participants in the parade by the coffin for the "viewing."

Psychologists would probably argue that it's part of the healthy dealing with grief and the death process. I surely desire not to be disrespectful where respect should be accorded, but I don't want to go on to whatever reward there is with people viewing my less than beautiful bod.

The most noble thing I could do would be to follow the example set by my late friend, Bruce Godfrey, who, in his words now, "donate my beautiful bod to the medical school at UNC in Chapel Hill for research."

If the medical schools have all the inventory they need when I go on, then the next most noble act would be simple and quiet cremation with the remains tossed off the Dawson's Creek Bridge here in Pamlico County, barring any demonstration from The Neuse River Foundation about polluting the waters.

Life is good when there can be both quiet reflection and laughter. So it should be for death.

Funerals are for the living. Don't give me a funeral. For those living on after me, let them get together for a few of my favorite things, barbecue and sweet tea, wine and cheese...and a big plate of collards.

My Creator is more interested in how I'm living, not what kind of "viewing" there might be after I become "the body."

Don't believe it? Ask Him?

And a parting shot—for any funeral—for anybody—anywhere—it's usually the weather that plays the most important role in how many mourners show up.

MAMA ALWAYS SAID,

during winter bad weather, "The closer to night it gets, the worse it's going to get."

TWENTY-THREE

MAKING FACES

A Methodist will speak to you if he meets you coming out of the liquor store. A Baptist will look the other way and hope there's no eye contact.

At one time I had the distinct pleasure of living across the street from the late and very great Hassel Matthews of Nashville, NC. Hassel was married to the greatest housewife that ever lived, Doreen, who could cook, sew and drive a pic'em up truck. Hassel was also known as the long time manager of the Nashville ABC store.

Hassel had more stories about people buying liquor than Carter had liver pills, back when the Carter company was still allowed to call 'em liver pills. Hassel told me once that he rarely sold a pint of liquor to anybody that was buying it for themselves.

Hassel said, "They'll come in here, scratch their heads like they can't remember something, and say, "Now what did he say to pick up for him?"

In the gentle South of yesteryear, genteel Southerners might not have wanted the general public to know they would take a drink of liquor, much less go to the liquor store and buy it.

Another quaint novelty about small town, rural America in the South is the genteel nature of taxi drivers like Dick Sills. He did more than transport those in need of transportation services. Baptist women were some of the most regular customers of Dick Sills, though they never set foot inside his old Chevrolet taxicab.

For them, a call to Dick was a summons to a delivery service. Dick's taxi stand was across the street from the liquor store in Nashville. His phone would ring, he would take the order across the street to Hassel Matthews and then deliver it to the "Baptist" who wouldn't think of letting anybody in town know that liquor was being consumed in their house.

Mentioning liquor was taboo. I wasn't conscious of this social phenomenon when I was afforded the great privilege and honor of offering a eulogy for Ted Garnett.

Ted Garnett, a British naval officer during the big one, WWII, was assigned to Washington, DC. There he met a true Southern belle, Elizabeth Strickland, from Nashville. (Remember, the real Nashville - - NC - - not TN.) Ted Garnett was known to visit me on July 4th, bearing champagne, waving the Union jack, and insisting I join him for a toast to King George III.

Ted Garnett could fondle the keys on an organ like no other. Elizabeth, a professional pianist, could do the same with the ivories on a piano. I sat in their parlor one evening, she on a grand in one corner, he on the organ in an opposite corner, as they played the then popular melody, "Feelings".

More feeling filled the spirits in that room that night than poetry or prose could translate. Here was a couple in the elder years of 70 plus, playing for the feelings of those decades younger.

Ted had both class and down to earth humor. He once paid a surprise visit to the law office of Tim Valentine. This was in those formative years for Tim Valentine, before he became the honorable member of the United States Congress who lived by a standard of ethics not customary for politicians.

(Is it any wonder that Tim retired from Congress rather than continue massively obscene fund-raising campaigns just so he could continue to be a politician?)

But the story is this. Ted approached Tim in a most serious manner. Here was an elderly man walking with a cane, proclaiming to his lawyer that he had heard that the old hotel in Nashville, which was situated on the same block as his classic, two story, front porch with columns home, was going to be used as a brothel.

Tim Valentine, lawyer extra-ordinaire, anticipated Ted's concerns and began talking of ways that legal action could be taken to protect the neighborhood. The gentleman Ted, a proper English gentleman, married to a proper Southern belle, from a fine family, inquired in the midst of Tim's attentiveness to his concerns,

"Tim, what do you think a season ticket would cost me?"

In Ted's eulogy, I was to end my remarks by inviting those present to leave the Nashville Methodist Church and walk two blocks to his home where his family would be serving a toast to his life.

I recall saying something to the effect, "Let us go forth from this place to raise a glass in honor of this man of class."

I later learned that it was pretty much unheard of in Nashville to mention raising a glass while standing in the pulpit of a church. Not realizing it at the time, I was simply doing what Tim did when he was a congressman, and that is, be yourself.

Ted Garnett was Ted Garnett.

We can put on different faces for different people, but the Great One in the Sky sees only the real face that we have. I've paid dearly to learn how to have just one face.

Ted Garnett, Hassel Matthews, and Tim Valentine offered the same face to The Force that they offered to everybody else.

TWENTY-FOUR

THEY ALL CAME AWAY MARRIED

Those who argue the case for style work harder at being recognized for style than substance. It's probably safe to say that for some, style is substance.

In the course of photographing hundreds of weddings for some two decades, I saw more effort put forth for style and image than that customarily witnessed by your average man on the street.

I photographed weddings that were royal galas, enough musicians to start a small orchestra, enough oysters, shrimp and fried soft-shell crab served at the receptions to feed a third world, developing nation for a week. A good deal of these society weddings cost the father of the bride more money than made by the average North Carolina citizen in one year.

I was always jealous that they would spend more money on flowers than on pictures. Flowers can wilt before the happy couple checks out for the honeymoon. Photographs, on the other hand, are the permanent record.

Nothing causes a MOTB, (that's wedding photographer terminology for mother of the bride) more stress than to think that either the recent or upcoming wedding of the Joneses might exhibit some little piece of style they haven't thought of for their daughter. If funerals are for the living, weddings are for the MOTB's. I had MOTB's come to my studio to look at extra pictures I might have from previously photographed weddings so they could allegedly see how certain colors of bridesmaids' dresses went with certain flowers. They were also searching for clues on how to outdo them in their own planning.

Don't judge me too harshly for being unduly cynical. One gets a tough skin after working at weddings just about every weekend for twenty years.

Now let's compare the high society nuptials with the less than high society.

I photographed one wedding in a small Ruritan Community Building where the groom wore his cowboy hat throughout the ceremony. I photographed some weddings so small and humble that I actually directed the affair, told the bridesmaids how to carry their flowers and pinned the boutonniere on the ushers. I photographed weddings where the bride and groom left in the groom's pick-em-up truck, his going away outfit consisting of blue jeans and a T-shirt.

I also photographed a couple of happy couples departing on the honeymoon in daddy's private jet.

In between, there were a lot of tasteful, simple dignified affairs that left everybody leaving the church feeling good about everything and everybody. That's contrasted with those where the two families were hardly speaking to one another because the mother of the groom was not happy with the role delegated to her by the MOTB.

Maybe I should point out that I photographed some weddings that bride and groom left the reception so drunk they hardly knew where they were. Maybe I should point out that I photographed some weddings that involved more scripture reading during the ceremony than a month of sermons. But those were the extremes, the exceptions, not the norm.

I photographed some weddings so tender and emotional, the groom cried more than anyone present. I photographed some weddings where the groom rushed the picture taking after the ceremony so he could get to the bar for a drink.

I saw bridesmaids faint, ushers pass out. I saw preachers be late. I saw a wedding cake on the floor of the reception hall after the caterer dropped it. I saw one church catch on fire—I photographed the bride hugging the firemen.

I could go on and on and on...but it gets to be more of a blur as more and more time passes between me and those twenty years of holding up a camera and saying, "Look happy now."

So what's my point? After all was said and done on the hundreds of different weddings with hundreds of different styles...the bottom line, in the eyes of the state sanctioning the preacher and in the eyes of the Creator of the human beings involved, they were all the same...they all came away married.

May not have stayed that way, but that's the way they left the church, or wherever they stood before a man with a Bible.

One final thought on weddings and wedding photography. I did it for twenty years, for the most part the luckiest man associated with the wedding. I felt genuinely a part of the family in many, many weddings. The days I came away disgusted were far outnumbered by the days I came away with the joy and satisfaction of having been a part of the most important day so far in the lives of two people.

And I want to personally thank people like Tommy Sasser of Nashville who had so many daughters. What a blessing for a wedding photographer!

Mama always said,

"A woman can throw out the back door with a tea-spoon more than the husband brings in the front door with a shovel."

For some shallow, pseudo-intellects, style is everything. The driving force in the life of such people is not substance, but style.

As a wedding photographer, I encountered a lot of style.

Brenda Stephenson, wedding director extra-ordinaire from Rocky Mount, NC, would often join me in irreverently imitating wedding guests gazing at vast arrays of nuptial styles. These guests would proclaim with enough syrup to stock a Karo warehouse, "That's soooo spesshhull".

Style doesn't often reflect substance. Hardly any pseudo-intellectual draped in style would expect to see either style or substance from a mobile home dweller. After all, there's no shortage of red-neck jokes about people who live in mobile homes.

I once lived in a mobile home. Wasn't the greatest habitat in the world, but it was also far from the worst.

At any rate, when one encounters a mobile home, often called a cracker box, painted up as a cracker box, rest assured—the inhabitants are people of style and substance—and lots of both.

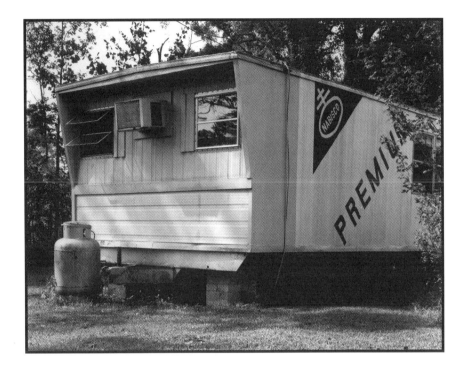

TWENTY-FIVE

COME AS YOU ARE

I got up this Sunday morning, wanting to go to church...but dreading wearing a tie in the heat of August. I wore the tie, sans coat. It made me think about Jesus and The Sermon on The Mount.

He simply preached to the multitudes that had assembled there. Theologians may dispute this, but I don't believe I've ever read an account in The Gospel about the multitudes running home to get their Sunday sandals on before The Master started to preach.

My guess is, every time Jesus preached to ever how many gathered, they gathered in whatever they were wearing without a lot of fuss about doing their hair and matching shoes with the outfit. I imagine the basic sandal of that period went with just about every type of robe or tunic or whatever you called those garments they wore that are pictured in all the children's Bible story books.

In my life as a wedding photographer, I once photographed nuptials that were so high Episcopalian that everybody there got a nosebleed. The head-celebrant-in-charge wore an outfit he must have bought at a Liberace garage sale. It was one of those few times in my life where I really practiced mature restraint. I did not go up to him as I wanted to and ask, "Is that the kind of garb Jesus wore when he preached?"

There's this old campfire song sung at church camps that's been around for ages. It sort of goes like this, "... Lord, I want to be like Jesus, in a my heart, in a my heart ..."

We do a lot of things in the worship of Jesus...that ain't like Jesus, things more cultural than scriptural.

I would bet that you could "Come as you are" to revival services at Harris Chapel.

My guess is, Jesus, or whatever Force there is up there, would
be happy for you to come, simply come…no matter how you are
when you come.

How you are when you come matters only to socially conscious
beings on this earth, not to the Great Spirit in the Sky.

That's not just a reality check, that's for real.

Twenty-six

Seeing Is Believing

Jerry Taylor, Ace Mechanic
Taylor's Gin Metropolitan District
Northern Nash County

Dear Jerry,

I've done it again. Been to the bushes and drug out another vehicle. Remember that Volkswagen I drug out of the bushes a few years ago, the one which costs me less to buy than it did to pay the title fees?

This time I drug out an old Isuzu Trooper. This little gem was auctioned off last March to satisfy a mechanic's lien for storage. Actually, it hadn't cost the mechanic too much to store it. He mowed around it for a couple of years, but didn't mow under it.

Jerry, do you think it was OK to buy a vehicle at an auction if I was the only one who showed up at the auction?

Jerry, should I be concerned that I bought this Trooper at auction last March and got to drive it home five months and nine days later?

Jerry, should I be concerned if the first time we got it cranked and running, the oil pressure gauge flopped down to about 9:30 while the temperature needle flipped over to about 2:30?

Jerry, should I be concerned if the mechanic called me on the coming home day to say, "Ben, it's ready, but we need to talk."

You know Jerry, Roosevelt said we had nothing to fear but fear itself, but I feared what this mechanic had to talk about. What does it imply when your ace mechanic says, "Ben, don't drive over 55 and I think it might be OK."

Jerry, what happens if I drive 56? Why did he keep saying he should have installed a big magnet underneath the thing to help keep the road free from falling debris?

This mechanic is a laid back kind of guy like you Jerry, but there are two main differences. His speakers without cabinets hanging from the framework of some shelves are wired to an old Radio Shack car radio which is wired to an old car battery and stays tuned to this area's classical music stations.

Not exactly Woodstock.

The other difference between you and him is that he always has a light at the end of a drop cord hanging from the hood of whatever car he is working on. Yep, he's handicapped. He can't see a thing without that light.

Back to the Trooper. Jerry, is it really alarming if he says for me not to take my eyes off the oil pressure gauge? And how bad is it if a vehicle hasn't been driven in three or four years?

I look at it this way. It surely didn't rack up a lot of mileage during that time. I mean, shouldn't we look for the positive in Troopers and in life?

As for driving this thing Jerry, I will remember what I read in the back of a church bulletin once, "A road with no stumbling blocks leads nowhere."

That being the case, I surely have been somewhere, and probably am headed somewhere else.

Jerry Taylor lives in the outskirts of Nash County, North Carolina. Though blinded by diabetes, is one hell of a mechanic.

He sees better, and more, than most people.

TWENTY-SEVEN

BODIES OR ENGINES...
PARTS ARE PARTS

Doesn't everyone know about the brilliance of surgeons?

They make hundreds of thousands of dollars per year. Yet, they are the golf and country club types for one reason and one reason only—blood washes off easier than grease. Consequently, they can clean up faster after work for a round on the links and dinner at the club.

Now here's why that's an accurate observation.

Back in college days, when I still had an impressionable mind, I recall very distinctly sitting in a sociology class taught by Dr. Robert Capps.

He shared the following observation with our

class, "The average automobile mechanic who fully understands the internal combustion engine is just as intelligent as the average surgeon who understands how to repair parts of the body. The workings of an internal combustion engine are just as complex as the parts of the human body."

My observation goes beyond the one made by Dr. Capps. I contend that the average automobile mechanic who understands what he's doing and why, has to possess a fair amount more intelligence than the average surgeon.

Let's take your average, run of the mill stomach. The great Creator is making stomachs today the same way he has made them for thousands of years. And you know what else, he's putting stomachs in exactly the same place in the human body he's been putting them for thousands of years.

Now people got all different kinds of things wrong with their stomachs and there's always new research on ways to repair all the different kinds of things wrong with stomachs, but the stomachs are all the same, in the same place, in all the human bodies.

But guess what I saw when "I saw the light" at a garage.

I saw Volvo's, Mercedes, Fords, Chevrolets, Toyota's, Honda's and one Isuzu Trooper with all the bushes pulled out of it. Some of those vehicles had carburetors, some had fuel injection, some had mechanical fuel injection, some had electronic fuel injection, some had distributor points, some had electronic ignition systems, some were gas engines, some were diesel engines, some had spark plugs, some did not use spark plugs.

Am I beginning to get my point across without having to go too much farther, or is that further?

Know what else?

All those parts that are just parts, they keep re-designing them from year to year and putting them in different places from year to year.

Now the surgeon, when he sees a room full of patients, he sees people with stomachs all original-ly made the same way and in the same place in all those little sweaty bodies waiting for hours on end to be called back to an examining room.

Now when all those people are well enough to leave the surgeon's office and drive their clunkers down to a garage, the mechanic sees every kind of engine, made every different kind of way you could imagine, put in as many different locations as pos-sible.

There's the transverse mounted, the straight six, the V-6, the V-8, the four cylinder, all hooked up to either automatic or straight drive transmissions, either two wheel or four wheel drive, front drive or rear drive.

If I have to go any further to make the point that a good automobile mechanic is just as intelligent as a surgeon, then you're not as bright as either a surgeon or a mechanic.

If we ever discover a way for grease to wash off as easily as blood, more mechanics will serve on the boards of more country clubs.

Is this a reality check or not?

Now let me make one thing clear, when my stomach hurts, I'm not going to a mechanic. On the other hand, I don't know too many surgeons who replace wheel bearings.

I respect them both for what they do...and I'm grateful for what they both do.

TWENTY-EIGHT

NOT ALL HEROES WEAR THEIR MEDALS

Nicki Potter was a mechanic and jack-of-all-trades.

Nicki worked mostly at Walter Banks' garage in Arapahoe. It was there that Nicki kept my bicycle running the whole year I delivered the newspaper on a four-mile rural route in 1960. It was there I spent most of my time talking to Nicki.

Nicki was a war hero. My granddaddy told me of one of his most talked about exploits during the big one, WWII. Nicki's outfit was in desperate need of a truck, so Nicki walked right into a German camp and drove one of theirs right out.

He lived to tell about, and be decorated for it.

There were many in Arapahoe who failed to remember Nicki's service to his country, they failed to remember that he fought for them to have free speech, the free speech they used to call him a "drunk."

Maybe that's why he drank.

I remember him saying one day, "I got a whole shit-pot full of medals over there in the house, but they don't mean a damn thing."

We all know they did mean something, even if he stored them in a shit-pot.

Garland Cahoon recently told me that many people were unaware that Nicki Potter had helped blow up a house housing German snipers—that the Germans had placed the snipers in an orphanage, thinking that Americans would not fire on an orphanage.

Nicki did not learn that it was an orphanage until he saw the bodies of children fly out the windows. Yes, some people drink too much because they have too much to forget.

I may have been young. But I wasn't too young to recognize a really special human being. I'm sorry that it's four decades later that I stand up to brag about knowing Nicki Potter.

He was an American hero who didn't wear pin striped suits. Retrospectively, more people should have realized that.

Twenty-nine

Don't Want No Dangling
Metal At The Wrong Time

The late, and somewhat great columnist from
Atlanta, Lewis Grizzard, shared my view about
men and earrings. Lewis pointed out that God created us men with seven holes in our bodies. I won't
write any more until y'all have had a chance to
count them. OK, got'em counted. I'll move on.

Lewis Grizzard said the only time he would be
willing for another hole to be poked into his flesh
would be if a doctor needed to get inside him with
some tube or whatever that would be crucial to saving his life. As someone who has so far survived
cancer, the subsequent surgery and radiation, I can
appreciate Grizzard's point of view.

I point out to every technician about to draw a sample from my arm, usually enough to meet the annual blood drive for the whole Southeastern United States, that I have one major allergy. I'm allergic to pain.

The truth of the matter is this. God created some beautiful bodies. Keep 'em clean, the hair brushed, maybe a little make-up on the womenfolk, and there's simply no need to dangle things from the ears or permanently paint up the skin to make the body any more beautiful. Come to think of it, it's down right arrogant to think that we frail humans can decorate ourselves better than God did.

On the other hand, while God don't make no mistakes, according to the poem, some things do go wrong with the cells that make up human bodies. Corrective surgery to correct an aberration, I can understand.

A normal ear is not an aberration. Why poke a hole in it?

Isn't it true that just about everything we do to make ourselves look better is done to make ourselves look better for the opposite sex? Aren't we trying to attract somebody that will ultimately want to crawl in bed with us? I know I didn't say that with a lot of delicacy, but isn't that more the truth than not?

Now I ask you, in the heat of passion, are you one

to be fondling earrings or caressing tattoos? I am a red-blooded American male. The red-blooded American female, just as she was created, is plenty good enough for me, even better than I deserve.

Aside from the fact that tattoos shouldn't be the source of heat in moments of passion, usually in dim light where you can't see the darn things anyway, there's another impracticality to tattoos. A tattoo design is permanent. A T-shirt with a wild design can be changed, hour-to-hour if the mood strikes. The really creative people, consequently, can express themselves using painted clothing with unlimited versatility as compared to those who lock themselves in to one design with permanently painted skin.

So, the truly creative, are the truly versatile. What's versatile about a permanent tattoo?

I'm well aware that a lot of truly creative people will condemn my view as narrow minded. Maybe there's a touch of Red Skelton in me. Red Skelton kept his act clean, telling no off-color jokes, always ending with "Good Night and God Bless." He once said that he would rather be called hokey than to be known for telling dirty jokes during family viewing times on TV.

Maybe I would rather be narrow-minded than run the risk of getting my teeth caught in tangled metal while...well, you know.

As weird as it may seem, I leave this little exposé of my narrow mindedness with this thought. I once took a kayak trip up to the very beginning of Dawson's Creek, several miles from the mouth of the creek where I live. John Hinners accompanied me, trying to teach me the finer art of paddling a kayak. At one point we were in total wilderness, nothing man-made within sight except the kayaks, and I guess our clothing.

The splendor of the verdant green landscape along the creek bank, the reflections in the glass-like water, the high cumulus clouds painted against a deep blue sky, all of this was just as it was created, not as it was tattooed. The human body, just as it was created, can be just as breath taking.

More than once, the human female body, just as it was created, has taken my breath away.

That may not really be a reality check, but it's surely for real.

THIRTY

NAKED OR NEKKID, THAT IS THE QUESTION

A lot of us are more nekkid than naked, especially in our state of minds.

Dennis Rogers, columnist for The News & Observer, a fish wrapper published in Raleigh, NC, has often delineated the difference between being naked or nekkid. If one is naked, one simply has no clothes on and is probably ready to take a shower. On the other hand, if one is in a nekkid state, one has no clothes on and is up to something, or is trying to get up for something.

Like Dennis Rogers, Hank Thoreau also made some philosophical observations about the state of having no clothes on. Thoreau pointed out that if a group of civilized men were in a room together, stripped of their clothes, there would be no way to discern who amongst them belonged to the most respected class.

Thoreau said, "It is an interesting question how far men would retain their relative rank if they were divested of their clothes."

Thoreau was counting on civilized people to learn something from his observation. In a nekkid state of mind, I could see people assigning rank to naked people.

Now believe it or not, I'm trying to take the high road here to a profound realization that designer clothes, high dollar tennis shoes promoted by mega-millionaire basketball players and luxury cars do not define the worth of a man's mind.

When I was a younger kid than the kid I am now, a pair of tennis shoes made by Converse was all anybody needed to play almost any kind of sport. But very few kids who played at any kind of sport when I was a younger kid than the kid I am now actually played tennis. Tennis was a little too high-brow for most of us country boys.

Where was I? Sometimes I get so distracted.

Oh, I was trying to make the point that one of our biggest shortcomings as a society is the way we judge someone by the clothes they wear or the car they drive. This whole business reminds me of the time when I was an undergraduate. It was the decade of the sixties and long hair on men was a novelty on my conservative campus at Atlantic Christian College.

One of my very best friends, Robbie Koelling, an English major and editor of the yearbook, had what was considered long hair for that period in time, the early part of the late sixties, i.e., early post first appearance by the Beatles. I recall someone asking him if he wasn't afraid that some of the more traditionally minded professors might be prejudiced negatively by his seemingly ever-growing mane.

Robbie said, and I remember it distinctly, "I have discovered that people don't really look at what you look like if you have something to say when you open your mouth."

I am confident that Thoreau was trying to get us to realize the value of a man by what he had to say, rather than what he had to wear. Robbie Koelling understood that.

Wouldn't you say that it is obvious to all the world that when we spend so much effort on what we wear, our minds are naked, to the point of being nekkid?

I bought a pair of tennis shoes the other day from a discount store for $24.99. I didn't pay 5 or 6 times that amount for designer shoes.

Thoreau might have been the only person impressed by such a move, or, realistically, unimpressed by whatever shoes one chooses to wear.

MAMA ALWAYS SAID,

"You're known by the associates your keep. You ought to go 'round with people that will lift you up, not bring you down."

THIRTY-ONE

ODE TO A ROMANTIC

I've been called a romantic, an idealist, but never a realist.

Robert Pirsig, author of *Zen and The Art of Motorcycle Maintenance*, tried to get us to understand that our lives should be a blend of the classical and the romantic.

According to Pirsig, the mind dominated by classical virtues was happiest maintaining a motorcycle, knowing the mechanical ends and outs of the machine from A to Z. On the other hand, the romantic is happiest riding.

Singer/songwriter John Denver died in a airplane that some would have called bike riding in the sky. I feel a personal sense of loss for a man who could write and sing lines such as, "You fill up my senses."

I feel a sense of loss for a man who could joyfully sing lines such as "Thank God I'm a country boy." I feel a sense of loss for a man who rode on The Calypso, the research vessel of Jacques Cousteau, then went on to sing about it with not only exuberance, but with reverence for the environment.

Television talk show hosts did their share of reviewing John Denver's life. It was said that John Denver had overcome many personal disappointments, that on the day he died, he was happy with himself.

It was also said that John Denver was a romantic.

In a final comment, one commentator said, "Oh, and the world can be so hard on romantics."

Romantics are hard on themselves. Romantics react first to what they feel, second to what they know.

I don't know what I am. I'm skeptical of labels. I may be a romantic, needing to understand a lot more about that engine strapped between my legs when I cruise the back roads of Pamlico County. There are very few front roads in Pamlico County.

It can take a while in one's life to balance knowledge with sensitive emotions and feelings. It was that balance that Pirsig sought and promoted.

As a romantic, John Denver communicated feeling, not necessarily musical notes.

Machines are hard on romantics. Machines help keep the world going. Romantics, with feelings, keep the world going in the right direction.

With respect for the work by Pirsig, thank God for country boys, romantics and John Denver.

John Denver was known the world over as a singer/song-writer...and as a romantic.

David Drake, MD, was known in and around the world of Fayetteville, NC, where he practiced medicine, and Oriental, NC, where he sailed the high seas of the Neuse River—as a romantic.

Nothing really separated their roles as romantics except the global fame that Denver acquired as a musician.

Both had more than one romance.

Both were sensitive, creative human beings.

Nothing John Denver did in his voyages with Jacques Cousteau could top the adventures of David Drake when Towboat US was often called to the rescue.

But the point is, one does not have to have achieved celebrity status in order for the blood of romanticism to transport the oxygen of life to the heart and soul.

THIRTY-TWO

ALL THAT CANDY ...
AND JESUS ISN'T DEAD ANYMORE

A cartoon on a Saturday before Easter in The Sun Journal, the daily fish wrapper published in New Bern, NC, showed a little girl dressed up in her finest dress ready for church. She is telling her mother, "I really like Easter Sunday. We get all that candy and Jesus isn't dead anymore."

Growing up in the South, one learns that death is an event of significant social importance.

When someone in your family died, everybody in the neighborhood brought over enough food to feed all the company that would come to visit. There would be enough pies and cakes to satisfy the sweet tooth of a small, third world developing nation.

Through the eyes of a child, we get all that food when a relative dies...but it's not possible to wake up the next day and say, "Granddaddy is not dead anymore."

I once worked at Nash Community College in Rocky Mount, North Carolina as a counselor. One of my colleagues, John Knight, put it all in perspective for us mortals.

More than once, I heard John say, in observing the passing of someone from this earth, "Death is so final."

Sidney Boone, retired minister, once told me, "Ben, with the help of God, go out and make this the best day of your life. It's the only day you have right now."

Put that within the framework of what John Knight observed, this is the only life we have right now. When I leave this life, nobody is going to say, "Ben isn't dead anymore."

This is the only chance we have right now. It's the most wonderful opportunity one could ever imagine. It's more than a little scary to see how we're going to pull it off...but the alternative is more than scary.

Handing an undertaker thousands of dollars to toss in a hole in the ground won't warm the chill of John Knight's cold observation. Neither will it give a second chance to make any day better than what it was.

This is the only day, the only life...any of us has right now.

Thirty-three

Boo!!!

Y'all know about the great wisdom of Marcus, don't you? Marcus Aurelius?

I have no earthly idea in the world who Marcus Aurelius was or is. Is he still with us, or is he like Elvis, making clandestine appearances at convenience stores?

At any rate, Marcus Aurelius is quoted in the very profound literary text of The Fisherman's Guide to Life by Criswell Freeman. Marcus says, "Our life is what our thoughts make it."

In a minute, that's a point I'm going to make about Halloween.

But first, let me tell you about the time I was almost thrown out of a movie theater. It was a

James Bond flick. By the way, I really like the way he says, "Bond's the name, James Bond."

Unlike most people, I see Bond flick's for what they are, comedies.

In this particular movie, I was laughing almost uncontrollably throughout the whole show. Needless to say, there were those around me who didn't think it was funny that a man could free-fall through the sky, catch a plane by its wing strut and fly it away. For me, that was funny beyond hilarious.

For me, that's what Halloween is, somewhat hilarious.

Remember Marcus? He said, "Our life is what our thoughts make it." Likewise, Halloween is what our thoughts make it. That's a lesson for those semi-crazy people who want to say that Halloween is some kind of Middle Ages un-Godly devil worship.

For those who want to make a big issue about Halloween being some kind of un-Godly affair, no five-year-old views Halloween as being either religious or anti-religious. No five-year-old attaches any kind of theological significance to Halloween.

Here it is in a one-word nutshell for everybody.

Halloween means one thing to children, C-A-N-D-Y. That's right—candy—the sweet stuff people buy and give away to kids who dress up in crazy costumes and knock on doors saying, "Trick or Treat."

No decent kid plans to trick anybody who doesn't

treat, even though he enjoys thinking about it. Thoughts are often more fun than actualities.

I remember Trick or Treating in Trent Court in New Bern a little over four decades ago.

I always told people I lived on Bern Street because I was ashamed to admit to the people who lived on the other side of town that I lived in Trent Court, a Federal housing project.

But what the hell, the truth is, as a youngster, I lived in Trent Court.

That's where I bagged a lot of candy, and that's where I learned that Halloween meant primarily one thing, a night to go out and get a lot of free candy simply by dressing crazy, knocking on doors and saying Trick or Treat.

Never, never ever, did I associate Halloween as being contradictory to anything I learned about life while attending Broad Street Christian Church. Halloween was—just as James Bond movies are—a comedy, but with the added benefit of bringing home a lot of candy.

There were a couple of exceptions. A few people would drop apples in the bag when approached by Trick or Treaters. That was not a lot of fun, no matter how healthy.

But one lady, one time when we were living in what were then the New Bernian Apartments...a brief reprieve from Trent Court...dropped quarters and dimes into the bags of Trick or Treaters.

Let me tell you. The only thing better than candy to youngsters is quarters and dimes. Of course, with the changing times, I guess the dimes have given way to dollars.

So don't tell me that Halloween is some kind of blasphemous, anti-religious, anti-Christian, pagan celebration. For the little old lady in New Bernian Apartments forty years ago, Halloween was sharing love with children.

Show me somebody who says sharing love with children is anti-religious, and I'll show you an idiot.

Life is what our thoughts make it. Halloween is what our thoughts make it.

Trick or treat?

Thirty-Four

Beauty, In The Eye Of The Behold-ee, As Well As The Beholder

I was just a few miles from home. It was late, after a long ride. A fleet-footed animal darted into my path and tragically confronted my tires.

Moving way too fast to be a coon, way too big to be a possum. I thought it might have been a fox. So intrigued was I with this possibly unusual road-kill, I drove back there in the daylight the next morning after breakfast just to see what kind of animal had had the misfortune to meet me on the road.

If you're wondering about me...you're no different from the 99.98887 % of the rest of the world's population doing the same thing, including myself. More than one person has said, "His bubble is off center."

I discovered I had accidentally killed a very beautiful, but very imposing creature of the wild, a bobcat. Having only seen a bobcat stuffed in a natural history museum, I did the morbid thing of bringing it home to photograph. Subsequent to the portrait session, I did accommodate the lifeless form a proper burial.

On the very same road, back in September, I came upon a large dead snake that had already met the fate of automobile traffic. Not black, as are 99.988875% of all snakes joining the ranks of the road-kills, this snake was brown with jagged black stripes.

Start wondering about me again.

I stopped to investigate and discovered a timber rattlesnake. I observed its head to see if it had a neck, the tell-tell sign of a pit viper. It did. A few rattles had survived the incident where the rubber met the road and the snake.

Would I have stopped to have looked at a black snake? Would I have driven back if I had known I had killed a possum? Would I have brought a possum home for a still life picture...very still life?

Certainly not!

Yet, God, in creating animals, all animals, possums and bobcats, black snakes and rattlers, must feel the same way about all of them. Somewhere there are lyrics, "Everything is beautiful, in its own way."

Thirty-five

And Grace Be Unto You

Back in the first century, a preacher by the name of Paul confused a lot of people with a sermon about heaven.

Paul told his flock that an application for admission to heaven listing a lot of good works would be no guarantee for approval. He said that one got to heaven only through the grace of God.

This is hard for us to understand in light of the fact that we live and breathe our lives on a different pattern of behavior. Study hard, get good grades; work hard, make money; practice hard, win on the playing field. Reward in every aspect of life usually follows good works.

I think Paul used the wrong kind of example to explain the power of God. Granted, there are no books in the Bible titled The Gospel According to Saint Ben.

Instead, let's recall the movie *Schindler's List.* Schindler convinced the tyrannical German at the concentration camp that real power could be exemplified in offering a saving grace, by sparing a life, rather than taking it.

Schindler persuaded the despotic German killer that not taking a life when one had the power to take a life, was a true exercise of power.

Perhaps that was what Paul was trying to explain about grace. God has the power to grant grace to those who seemingly don't deserve it. Paul was not trying to diminish the value of good work.

People, as well as God, have the power to offer grace.

Grace is something that we have all received, from God, and from our fellow man. Perhaps that is something for which we should stop and be thankful. How many times have we deserved a fate worse than what we received? How many times have we been spared by grace, offered either by God or our fellow man?

I have written many Thanksgiving columns for various newspapers over the past two decades, offering thanks for everything from sunsets to a plate of collards. Perhaps, it is time to give thanks for something not as tangible as a turkey making the ultimate sacrifice for a big meal.

Perhaps it is time to give thanks for grace, undeserved from either our Creator or our fellow man.

THIRTY-SIX

WHEN THE HEART SEES MORE THAN THE EYE

This is a story about love and respect.

Of the hundreds upon hundreds of weddings I photographed over two decades, perhaps one epitomized love and respect more than all the rest.

And guess what? I'm not talking about the passion between bride and groom.

I was hired to photograph a wedding in Raleigh...the home of the real zoo in North Carolina, the state legislature.

Prior to this event I had photographed quite a few of the "high society" weddings in Rocky Mount. Daughters of doctors and entrepreneurs had served up receptions that served up fried soft shell crabs for hundreds of guests.

This wedding in Raleigh was truly elegant. The reception was held at a historic home now used primarily for only the most dignified of social affairs. Reception music was provided by a string ensemble. Guests were tastefully served by roving tuxedoed caterers.

Got the picture? This was not your typical Saturday afternoon hoedown.

Although a Saturday afternoon hoedown ain't too bad a thing to go to either.

Now let's back up and give a few details in capsule form that I learned throughout the course of the afternoon.

The bride had grown up on a rural Iowa farm. She had made quite a name for herself in the corporate world in Texas before moving to the Raleigh-Durham area to work with a large corporation there. Many of the wedding guests were old friends from Texas.

The groom was an insurance executive. He was no po boy, i.e., he won't poor.

Yet despite their career successes, both bride and groom exhibited a touch of class in human qualities that I think would be hard to match. They were both genuine and sincere personalities.

When I arrived at the church, the bride gave her most specific instruction of the entire afternoon.

She informed me that she had arranged for her mother and father to arrive via limousine. As Iowa farmers, her parents had never ridden in a limousine. I was to be standing on the curb when they arrived to photograph this historic moment for them.

I was there at the appointed hour. A limousine so long that it could barely make the turn onto the two-lane street where the church was situated pulled up right beside me. Camera and flash were ready.

First out was a short man almost as round as he was tall in a black tuxedo, obviously the father. He didn't stand out too much as being different, but those white socks with the black tuxedo stood out like a bolt of lightening streaking across a black sky.

He held the door for the mother of the bride, MOTB in wedding terms, who emerged wearing a plaid, double knit, God-awfully ugly two-piece leisure suit.

Guests at this wedding were so highbrow that I bet this was the first time they had ever seen a double-knit, plaid, two-piece leisure suit.

But they saw it that afternoon because that bride, delightfully and proudly, introduced her mother and father to all—all of the guests.

This man and woman were her parents. White

socks and a leisure suit did not impair her love and respect for them at her very elegant wedding.

That's love and respect of the highest order.

And that's a reality check for those who confuse style with substance.

THIRTY-SEVEN

WHERE'S THE SKY

O nce, in the world of commercial photography, a Hasselblad lens messed up on me right before a wedding.

"Messed up" is vernacular for malfunctioned.

In my state of desperation before leaving for the wedding, Sidney Boone appeared at my door just for a brief chat.

Noting my advanced state of falling to pieces, he inquired as to the nature of my anxiety.

I tried to explain my futile situation.

He walked to the door, opened it, looked up...and asked...

"Ben, is the sky falling?"

Ummm, these reality checks keep rolling along.

Thirty-Eight

Murder In The Wild

When I was about 12 or 13, I got my first shotgun, a .410. Not long after I graduated to a 12 gauge, at that time, the typical cannon used in artillery barrages against deer.

Man—did I feel like a man—standing out there in frozen weeds, my feet needing a lot more than the one pair of socks I had worn.

In the few times I went hunting around Arapahoe, I saw only one deer within range, froze like the weather while another hunter took him down. Consequently, I never even took a shot at one. I felt disappointed then.

I'm elated now that not a single graceful, beautiful animal died at my unsteady hands.

In an earlier life when I was in the picture frame business, the daughter of one of the biggest hunters around brought in a post card for me to frame. The picture on the card was that of two buck deer driving a car with a dead hunter strapped to the hood, in exactly the same fashion that hunters often drive around with their victim tied down so the public can view their conquest of what was once free in the wild.

I think this particular national association that tries to influence elections in this country by favoring conservative politicians who will cling to any emotional issue that sounds good—but is not really good—must be made up of insecure men. They have to be insecure if they think amassing great quantities of weapons of mass destruction so they can pretend to be Daniel Boone and bring home supper makes them feel more secure.

I'm going to let the whole world in on a big secret.

Guess what? It's not necessary to go out like Daniel Boone and risk killing somebody while invading private property to take a shot at a beautiful deer that won't taste good no matter how many onions are cooked with it to hide the wild taste. We now have super-markets with fresh meat that's been grain fed so it won't have the wild taste.

I realize the macho-instinct will still exist. Some men feel better if they actually kill the supper themselves.

I got a suggestion for you. If you follow this suggestion, no free and beautiful wild animal will suffer unnecessarily. There is virtually no chance you will irritate property owners as you make the kill. There is virtually no chance that a stray bullet will fell a friend, family member or unknown innocent victim.

Get a job in a chicken processing plant or a hog slaughter house. You can kill animals all day that will do a lot better job of feeding your family than some wild animal that tastes like all the wild things it has eaten in the woods.

Better still, to really eat healthy, do as I do, go fishing. There is the chance you might drown. But better you drown than kill an innocent victim with a stray bullet. Or...better you drown than to kill a beautiful deer just so you can cut its rack of antlers off for bragging rights while you let the meat go to waste.

I don't fish for the sport of it. I fish, hoping to catch a speckled trout that will be supper.

I have a real problem with people who hunt or fish and call themselves sportsmen. Daniel Boone was not a sportsman. He was simply a pioneer, hunting wild game to survive. Had there been a corner grocery store near the cabin, I'm confident Daniel Boone would have been happy not to have gone hunting for supper.

There's a world of difference between hunting because it's a sport and hunting because it's necessary.

That difference is the difference that separates a civilized man from an uncivilized man.

MAMA ALWAYS SAID,

"Wash your face with cold water before going out in the cold. It'll close up your pores and not let the cold in so you can't catch cold as easy."

Thirty-nine

Creative Taxidermy

What do you think of men who hunt for big game or big fish so they can have it mounted to hang on their living room wall?

They are slaughtering a creature of the Creator which is no threat to them, merely for bragging rights.

I don't want to sound too "preachy" here, but how do you think the great Creator feels about one of his creations killing another of his creations, not for need or survival, but for the sport of it.

If evolution is the process of creation, what if black bears overtake human beings in the "creationary" chain. How would a hunter with an orange cap look mounted on the wall of a bear's cave? Which would fade first, the taxidermy job on the hunter or the orange dye in the fabric of his hat?

Hey, I just thought of something. Why do we waste thousands of dollars in this idiotic funeral process of embalming people? Why don't we take our dearly departed loved ones to a taxidermist, have them mounted and sit 'em up in their favorite chair. I bet mounting by a taxidermist would last longer than embalming.

Put hinges in their joints and you could stand them up or sit them down in their favorite chair.

I can see it now. Over here on the wall is a big blue marlin I caught last summer off Hatteras. Over there in the chair is my dad who taught me to fish.

That would save a lot of real estate we waste on cemeteries trying to save something that really isn't saved.

Aren't cemeteries a way for people to mount people much the same way people mount beautiful animals on their living room walls?

The mounting of what once was...is kind of futile.

FORTY

AND IT'S CHRISTMAS?

I know young folks are tired of hearing older folks talk about what it was like when they were young folks.

I am not that old. At least I've never told tales of walking a mile through deep snow to get to school...because I didn't.

Whether you're tired of hearing it or not, here goes. Way back when I was younger kid than the kid I am now, if we had good weather on Christmas, every yard was filled with youngsters playing with new toys. Kids were out sporting new basketball goals, footballs, bicycles or roller skates.

Really telling my age, I grew up when it was quite fashionable for little boys to be out playing cowboys and Indians with toy cap pistols. That was back in the middle of the last century.

Those boys with a few more years on them had BB guns. I'm not so sure they were constructive gifts. Sparrows and other lgb's (lgb's are little gray birds) often fell prey to the better shots.

I had a hard time shooting straight but I was good enough to hit the tin roof of the old maid's house who lived next door. The object was to fire off a couple of rounds, stash the gun, get on the bicycle and clear out so you could claim you weren't even home when she came over to complain to Mama.

As dastardly as they were, BB guns at least were outdoor toys.

About three years ago, on a sunny and warm Christmas Day, driving a round trip of 34 miles to visit Mama in the nursing home, I passed only three houses with children outside playing with an outside toy.

One little girl, with a mama's help, was trying out a new pogo stick. One little toddler was sporting a new John Deere tractor tricycle. Two little girls were apparently trying out new roller blades on their driveway.

Think about that people. Thirty-four miles of houses is a lot of houses, even if this is rural Pamlico County. Where were the kids? What did they get for Christmas? They surely didn't get toys to take out to the great outdoors.

How will children ever appreciate this beautiful planet if they never see it, if they never experience it, if they never feel it wrapped around them?

Where were the kids?

They were most likely inside playing computer games or listening to new stereos. They could have been trying on new clothes.

But instead of listening to a stereo, think about the concert that birds give, backed up by an orchestra of rustling pine boughs conducted by gentle breezes.

Near the river, what about the never-ending symphony of waves lapping the shoreline?

Boring you say...hell no!

The concerts staged outdoors are breathtaking...and thankfully forever playing over and over without having to push buttons to change stations. The stations change as the sun moves about through the universe, the wind shifting clouds as frequently as the tempo shifts from one piece of music to the next.

Children might see pictures of outdoor drama on a color monitor, but they won't experience it...they won't feel it.

What's wrong with being outdoors and falling down in a mud hole? What's wrong with skinning knees sliding down a tree trunk?

What about just walking through the woods, jumping ditches, encountering new discoveries since the last rain or windstorm? What about the thrill of a covey of quail scaring the daylights out of you as you surprise them walking through a field of tall grass?

Children who grow up not feeling things that are beautiful and wonderful in this world...I fear...might grow up without feelings.

I still can't get over it. I rode thirty-four miles. I passed house after house on a glorious spring-like day served up for Christmas. And yet, only three houses were adorned with children playing outside with new Christmas toys.

There's something wrong with this picture.

FORTY-ONE

HAS HE FINISHED???

Mama had her share of wisdom packed away, but she had a hard time understanding that crazy people could be intelligent. Some people have a difficult time understanding that uneducated people can be intelligent. Conversely, some educated people are not intelligent, and may or may not be crazy.

On the other hand, some people with only modest intelligence, either with or without education, are very smart.

Mama grew up when education was synonymous with intelligence. We know that correlation ain't so now, don't we?

We also know that knowledge and wisdom are not

inter-changeable.

I have this fantasy that someday I will get invited to speak at a high-falutin' graduation at a prestigious university. After my introduction, which would be short, listing a very short list of credits, I stroll to the podium, knowing full well everybody out there in the land of pomp and circumstance is dreading a long and perhaps boring speech.

Here follows my speech, every bit of it.

Education and intelligence are not one and the same thing.

Knowledge and wisdom are not one and the same thing.

Legal and ethical are not one and the same thing.

Education, intelligence, knowledge, wisdom, legal and ethical. Of these, the greatest are wisdom and ethical.

And don't forget what I saw on a bumper sticker, "The truly educated never graduate."

Act accordingly.

Thank you.

Think anybody would remember that speech? Reckon the university would stop payment on the check they gave me for an honorarium?

As Robert Fulghum would say, "Maybe, maybe not."

FORTY-TWO

WHEN EGGS HAD TRADING POWER

Where is one's life headed when surprise Sunday afternoon visitors knock on your door, introduce themselves, and then say they came to meet and greet your dog?

As Dave Barry would say, "I am not making this up."

I was sitting out on my dock washing fishing tackle. I'm probably the only soul who washes plastic grubs. I tie them to the end of the line on my rod and reel, toss 'em in the creek and slowly reel 'em in. To the casual observer it would appear that this activity would constitute the act of fishing. But if I don't claim to be fishing, I don't have to be embarrassed about not catching anything.

At any rate, in the course of washing a plastic grub, a stately gentleman arrives and introduces himself as Grady McCotter. He and his lovely wife had driven down to meet Daisy, star of a recent column I scribed for the New Bern, NC Sun Journal.

After Daisy had gotten in her licks with the guests, Mr. McCotter and I engaged in that truly Southern ritual of determining how many mutual friends we had, who's daddy was who, who was kin to whom, and that favorite Southern topic, "the good old days."

We talked about all the farmers I had worked for when I was a younger child than the child I am now. It seems that in an earlier life, Mr. McCotter had sold a green tractor to just about every farmer in Jones, Pamlico and Craven Counties.

Our inventory of friends covered the Hardison boys, Fred, Tuffy and Rob. All were on my paper route when as a young entrepreneur, I sought fame and fortune delivering The Sun Journal. What I found at Rob Hardison's house one Christmas was better than fame or fortune.

It was cold and dark when I arrived at the Hardison house that Christmas almost four decades ago. Some people on the route that night tipped me either a dime or a quarter since it was

Christmas. But at Rob's house, I heard him say from inside, "Is that the Casey boy? Tell him to come on in and sit down here at the table."

I went on in and sat down at the table. To warm me up for the two-mile ride back to Arapahoe, I was served homemade biscuits topped with homemade strawberry jam and rich, real cream from the cow out in Rob's barn. I started to say homemade cream because the Hardisons had separated it from the milk of their own cow. But giving credit where credit is due, the cow did make the cream.

For a paperboy, that kind of treatment from a customer is, borrowing a line from the Jack Nicholson movie, "as good as it gets."

Those were the days when the house I lived in didn't even have a telephone. But I really didn't know I was poor. Being poor and trying to "out poor" everybody else who has ever been economically challenged was the subject of a recent AC Snow column in The News & Observer, a fishwrapper of some notoriety published in Raleigh, NC. Snow recalled a meeting with other journalists in which each laid claim to growing up the poorest.

AC told about growing up in the depression in Surry County. His allowance was one egg per week from the henhouse which he could take to the store and trade for a sucker.

My grandfather let me have a whole dozen eggs at

the time. He told me to take them out to one of the stores in Arapahoe and trade them for a loaf of bread. AC, I didn't get a sucker, but I once ate five banana sandwiches in one sitting.

Mama said I was going to ruin my stomach...and I did.

I believe Einstein would proclaim that theories about being poor are really theories of relativity.

When all is said and done, I would love to undo a lot of what I've done in my life.

On the other hand, I wouldn't trade for anything those days of bartering eggs for a loaf of bread.

The McCotters helped me remember the truly good of the good old days.

Taking with us the reality that we can't stay long, sometimes it's really nice to go back.

FORTY-THREE

LUNCH:
TWO BISCUITS IN A TIN PAIL

Emmy told me that she read about a new lunch box for school children that could be plugged in to an electrical outlet to heat up the several course meal inside.

My, my. What will they think of next?

I made a special trip to visit Mama at the nursing home to ask her what she carried for lunch walking a mile through deep snowdrifts in the late 1920's.

It rarely snows here in extreme Eastern North Carolina, but like all Mama's tales of walking to school, it was always through those deep snow-drifts.

Mama said she carried her lunch to school in a

small pail, a metal bucket that had been the container for Karo Syrup. Other children, she told me, employed a lard pail as a lunch box.

In that little Karo Syrup pail, her standard fare for lunch was two biscuits, one with meat, one with preserves.

She said, "We always had plenty of meat at breakfast, either ham or sausage. My mama would pack a biscuit with whatever meat we had for breakfast that day, plus a biscuit with preserves, usually pear preserves."

I asked her if that was all. She said that was it. In her last year at Arapahoe High School, students could purchase a cup of hot chocolate for a nickel to go with their lunch.

This was the generation that became the parents of the people who put a man on the moon. If they did that by walking a mile to school through deep snow drifts carrying a Karo Syrup pail holding two biscuits for lunch, heavens to Betsy, where will the children of the generation of plug-in lunch boxes put a man?

Mars? Jupiter? Or the corner video store?

FORTY-FOUR

TODAY'S CHILD

The world is coming to an end.

Well, yeah, we all figure that it might do that some day, but now I know for sure.

My eight year old step-grandson, Matt, spent seven days in our house, under our care. He was born in North Carolina, has lived all his life in North Carolina, mostly in Alamance County, and not in downtown Burlington either.

Now that I think about it, maybe all that construction on I-85/I-40 around Burlington may have created the personality that surely foretells the end of the world. The construction probably started about the time of his birth. On the other hand, I'm a half century old plus, and I think they have been working on the Interstate around Burlington and Greensboro, North Carolina since I found out there was a Burlington in North Carolina as well as Vermont.

At any rate, here's the scoop on why I know the world is coming to an end.

I offered to cook the kid some collards, gore-may greens, fed to me by Mama since I graduated from baby food. That's the brain food that has made me what I am.

Guess what that kid said to me!

What are collards?"

Now think about it. This kid is North Carolina born and bred, in Alamance County. What's happening to the quality of Southern culture in Alamance County?

But it gets worse.

I bought a Bogue Sound watermelon, chilled it at the expense of throwing out half of what was in the refrigerator.

Bogue Sound is that body of water separating Morehead City from Atlantic Beach, NC. Watermelons grown on the mainland along the shores of Bogue Sound have the same celebrity status as maple syrup from Vermont or peaches from Georgia.

But what does Matt announce to all the world?

"I don't like watermelon."

It gets worse. I cooked scrambled eggs, bacon and toast for breakfast one morning. You know what that kid wanted to put on scrambled eggs? Ketchup!

Now I've heard of damnyankees putting ketchup on scrambled eggs, but who would have ever pictured an eight-year-old boy from Alamance County in North Carolina putting ketchup on scrambled eggs.

Not me. that's for sure.

It gets worse. Here on the mighty shores of the Neuse River in Pamlico County at Dawson's Creek, we awoke one morning to find crabs so eager to be caught that they hung around the dock pilings inviting capture by the dip net, not even bothering with the bait in the crab pots. About lunchtime we had a big mess of crabs caught so we proceeded to cook and clean them. All of this fervent activity took its toll on the kid. He announced that he was hungry while the water was just beginning to heat for the crab boil.

[Do I need to explain what a mess of crabs is? Around here, a mess of something is not necessarily something that has been messed up. Mess is a quantitative noun indicating a good plenty of something, a bountiful serving and so forth and so on. For example, one might say to one's neighbor, "I'm going fishin' this afternoon and if I catch a good mess, I'll bring you over a mess to fry for supper."]

Well, we offered that great American staple, a peanut butter and jelly sandwich, to tide him over until the crabs were cooked and picked clean from the shells. Had some of that apple jelly made by the Texas Pete folks over in Winston-Salem, not Texas, and a childhood favorite, crunchy peanut butter by Jif.

Like I warned, it gets worse.

He wandered back into the kitchen while I was sweating, not perspiring, over the pot of boiling crabs. He held up the sandwich with about two mouthfuls eaten and proclaimed with disdain, "There's peanuts in this peanut butter."

It took me a while to unravel that mystery. He didn't like crunchy peanut butter, he wanted smooth.

Now let's take inventory.

A North Carolina boy, eight years old ...

1. Doesn't know what collards are.
2. Doesn't like watermelon.
3. Puts ketchup on scrambled eggs.
4. Doesn't like peanut butter with peanuts in it.

The world is coming to an end.

FORTY-FIVE

WISDOM FROM
THE BROOM CLOSET

Seen the bumper sticker, "Let me tell you about my grandchildren."

Well, let me tell you about my grandfather.

I lived with my grandfather for five years. I was eleven when I moved in with him in the very rural village of Arapahoe in Pamlico County. I had been living in New Bern just 21 miles away. Because of that, I was always a city slicker to him, a big disappointment for me.

My grandfather, after selling his small farm, after using all the proceeds to pay the medical bills when my grandmother had spinal meningitis, took a job as the janitor at Arapahoe Elementary School. He was truly a stoic figure, a dry sense of humor, a little bit of a storyteller, and more honest than most could ever hope to be.

I was never intensely close to my grandfather. When I knew him best, he was quite elderly, I was quite young. He thought me not good enough to be a country boy. When I came home with a good report card, he always said, with no emotion in his voice, "A is for average, B is for bad."

I have had a hard time deciding about the memory I should have of him. I got help from a man who knew him when he was the janitor at the school. This man is now a counselor at Pamlico Community College.

I saw Floyd Hardison today. His daddy drove big trucks when I was living in Arapahoe. I got to watch Walter Banks rebuild the engines in them at his garage in Arapahoe. (That's just a little more nostalgia thrown in for free.)

Floyd Hardison told me today, "You know, back when Mr. Ben was our janitor, nobody ever heard of schools in Pamlico County as having guidance counselors. But Mr. Ben was better than any guidance counselor. Every boy at that school knew Mr. Ben. He diffused playground disputes and told stories that helped everybody solve their problems. Kids went to him with real questions, more than they went to teachers."

School systems need to really look at who they hire to do traditionally menial tasks. Some good can be done there that is not menial.

FORTY-SIX

A LIGHT ON EVERY TWIG

There's too much Christmas in religion.

Now you're saying to yourself, where's this guy coming from. After reading that statement, descendants of citizens who used to drape themselves in white sheets and parade through the country at night are probably running out to soak some timber in kerosene from which they can erect a cross in my front yard.

But read on before you set fire to the cross and throw rocks through my front windows.

Much is written and proclaimed every year about the over-commercialization of Christmas by retailers. Christmas ornaments hit the display racks before the orange and black of Halloween have faded. Trendy gift shops in yuppie vacation resort areas actually promote themselves as selling Christmas paraphernalia all year long.

And Christmas lights.

Great day in the morning. I remember my tender college years of living in Wilson, North Carolina. That city started a tradition of decorating homes by placing one single white electric candle in each window. Now I don't want to appear to be one of those types who can say "marrrrvvvvelous" with my nose so far up in the air that I would drown on a foggy morning, but that was a "marrrrvvvvelous" sight to see riding down Nash Street, the city's main thoroughfare, at night.

Now, I understand that the Raleigh branch of the state's public university system, called North Carolina State University by those enrolled there, has a whole new graduate program with an emphasis on the study of stress to trees and shrubs caused by an over-abundance of electric wires strung on them at this time of year. There is also the concern that the extra hours of luminosity during November and December might upset the biological clock of plant life. The early blooming out in cold winter months due to extra artificial daylight hours could create a potential for plant damage.

Now if you take that last paragraph literally, your

brain has been affected by the light radiating from the trees and shrubs. But you do get my drift, don't you? I grew up at a time when Mama made us cut the lights off on the tree inside the house early at night to save on the light bill. There were no lights strung on the cedar tree which looked like a giant Christmas tree near the back kitchen door.

For those of you too young to know, the light bill is the electric bill. I am old enough to remember houses that electricity did one thing, power light bulbs. Consequently it was the light bill. Yes, I remember having an ice box, in which perishable food was kept cold by huge blocks of ice delivered every other day or so by an ice man.

Wait a minute, I was supposed to be writing about too much Christmas in religion. How did I get way off onto all this other stuff?

Let's wrap it up in a hurry.

Christmas celebrates the birth of Jesus Christ. But what about all that He taught to the world about man's relations with God and man's relations with man during his short ministry on this earth?

Why do churches have all these celebrations, The Hanging of the Greens, an event where every windowsill and structure in the sanctuary that will support a poinsettia is granted the opportunity to do just that? There are cantatas that boast songs that are not the traditional Christmas carols which most of us can understand. There are mid-night communion services. There are the traditional nativity scenes. And in recent years there is the trendy living Christmas tree whereby the cantata is performed by persons who can endure being a part of a human pyramid.

Now this is all well and good, but...where are the special ceremonies or holidays celebrating The Sermon on The Mount, the miracles, and the profound lessons taught by The Master through the use of parables.

Jesus packed a whole lot of preaching and teaching between His birth and His crucifixion. What holidays celebrate the highlights of his teaching? There are special holidays recognizing His birth and His death, but not His teachings.

Well, for one thing, the birth and crucifixion are certainly more applicable for dramatic productions and commercial applications.

It would be more appropriate on Christmas Eve to turn to The Sermon on The Mount and read to the family, "Happy are those who are merciful to others, God will be merciful to them."

Have mercy!

FORTY-SEVEN

SAVE THE TREES—NO MORE CHURCH BULLETINS

I went to church today.

I followed the service through a two-page bulletin that had a title for just about everything said and done.

There was a prelude, a tolling of the hour, hymn of the hour, a response to the hymn of the hour, a responsive reading using a psalm as a text, an invocation, a moment for fellowship, a time for prayer concerns for the sick and afflicted, a prayer hymn, an anthem by the choir, a scripture reading, the sermon, a hymn of response, the offering, an invitation to communion, a communion hymn, prayers of the elders, partaking of the bread and the cup, the benediction, and finally, the benediction response, a little verse sung by all.

That's when the pews take on the same characteristic as the starting blocks in Olympic time trials for the hundred-yard dash. The dash at this moment is to the car and lunch.

This kind of scenario is repeated in just about every protestant church in the land, in some shape, fashion or form every Sunday.

Not only that, to facilitate the ceremonies, most churches have elaborate sound systems. Some have expensive lighting for dramatic productions. I am not criticizing, but let's face it, church sanctuaries have become elaborate, electronically operated playhouses for theater productions.

Now, for the most famous, for the greatest sermon of all time, The Sermon on the Mount, according to the Book of Matthew, Jesus saw the crowds and went up a hill where he sat down. The disciples gathered around him and He began to teach.

I want to know how Jesus was able to have such an impact on so many people without a sound system and without ushers passing out a bulletin with a multiplicity of program notes.

What a shame that preachers today can't just sit down and get the multitudes to gather around for some simple teaching!

That's reality check 101.

FORTY-EIGHT

HOW CHURCHILL
LED ENGLAND TO VICTORY

Recently, I made a foray into one of my Robert Fulghum books, It Was On Fire When I Lay Down On It. Fulghum, who proclaimed in his first book that he learned everything he needed to know in kindergarten, has written philosophical humor under a variety of titles, such as Uh-Oh and Maybe, Maybe Not.

As for myself, I haven't yet learned all I need to know.

Although I was looking for information about publishers when I pulled his books off the shelf, I soon discovered I had insight into the New Year and New Year's resolutions. You know, we often find

something more important than what we were looking for that wasn't what we were looking for.

Things happen for a reason.

In the first chapter of It Was On Fire When I Lay
Down On It, Fulghum relates a story in which res-
cuers raced into a building which was spewing
forth smoke from an upstairs window. Upon break-
ing into the apartment, they found a man lying on
a smoldering mattress. Once the fire was extin-
guished, firemen naturally inquired about how this
happened.

The man replied, "I don't know. It was on fire
when I lay down on it."

Fulghum goes on to say that the victim's observation is really a life story in one sentence.

As for New Year's resolutions, we have made so
many promises to ourselves and to others in the
past, yet we keep right on jumping out of the frying
pan into the fire. In other words. we try to fly kites
in thunderstorms when we know full well we are
not Ben Franklin.

Fulghum made a number of other observations
about repetitive patterns of behavior that leave us
gasping on the smoke from the bed that was on fire
when we chose to lie down. For example, he told the
story of the man who, day after day, complained to
his fellow workers about having to pull from his
lunch box, the same old boring sandwich. So natu-

rally, he was asked who made his lunch.

The man replied, "I do."

Biblical scripture indicates that we have good company in this dilemma of repeating into each New Year patterns of behavior that lure us to sleep on smoldering mattresses. Saint Paul is reported to have said, "I cannot understand my own behavior. I fail to carry out the things I want to do, and I find myself doing the very things I hate."

Fulghum observed that psychiatrists had made a good deal of money from people with this dilemma, while at the same time theologians had made a lot of noise. He also observed that this was a dilemma that afflicted every one of us.

I choose to take a more optimistic view than that left in the first chapter of Fulghum's book. He left me with the feeling that he thought we were helpless in this quest to stay out of burning beds. He didn't say anything about those of us in the elusive search for a burning bed.

Wait a minute, wait just a damn minute. Before you go off where you not supposed to go with that last comment...we're talking philosophical life choices here, not dens of passion.

Now it is time to remember, not Robert Fulghum, but Winston Churchill. That great statesman said that he was an optimist, that he didn't see much use in being anything else.

With the full knowledge of Fulghum's observation that we humans can't stay out of burning beds, I choose to enter the New Millennium with Winston Churchill's optimism.

I don't see much use embarking any other outlook.

FORTY-NINE

QUALIFYING TO BE A NAVY SEAL

A ndy Polo and George Benedict cared about their friend, Ben.

Ben's studio and home had been flooded twice by Hurricane Dennis in September of 1999. The roof on his house had been declared a total loss after Hurricane Floyd, just two weeks after the last blow of Dennis.

Andy called Ben late one afternoon in October and told him to be at the Dawson's Creek boat ramp in fifteen minutes. He and George were going to take him for a boat ride across the Neuse River to Adams Creek, the Atlantic Intra-Coastal Waterway, on to Morehead City, NC for dinner.

The 48-minute ride over on the powerboat had

been uneventful except for the genuine pleasure of riding across rivers and creeks to the ocean port of Morehead City for dinner.

Andy docked the boat at a waterfront restaurant where subsequently a most exquisite seafood meal was served to the trio on the deck adjacent to the dock. It was outdoor dining at its finest.

Ben was truly humbled by the genuine bond of friendship exhibited by George and Andy, especially after they paid the tab for one hell of a meal.

As dusk dawned over the waterfront, George politely and respectfully suggested that it might be wise to begin the return trip after just one more beverage.

Getting back down the "big ditch", also know as the inland waterway, back to the Neuse River, across the river and into Dawson's Creek was not something to be taken lightly, even in broad daylight.

Now Ben appreciates the friendship of Andy as much as anybody could appreciate friendship.

Keep in mind, Andy has spent many hours on the water, and has made this particular trip many times before—in daylight.

Should Ben have been worried after they passed under the big bridge to cross the Newport River and Andy asked, "Which way do we go here?"

Then Ben discovered that Andy had no spotlight

on his boat.

There is profound dialogue amongst the three as they attempt to determine what is and what is not an island in the river. Trying to negotiate the sea-lanes, looking for the entrance to the "big ditch," intense onboard negotiations begin as to whether red markers should be on the right or the left for the return trip north on the intracoastal.

It's now dark.

No moon—as in the actual night of the new moon—you know, total darkness.

Andy has the traditional green starboard running light, the port red running light—but no spot light for finding and identifying channel markers.

His console lights lighting the depth finder and rpm's seem to blind him with his bifocals.

When he turns off the console lights so they won't blind him, the running lights go out—in other words—like you know—invisible to other water traffic.

Then George, a sailing veteran, says to Ben, "What color is that marker light ahead?"

Ben, wondering to himself, wonders, "What the hell do you mean, what color is that marker light?"

George replies, "I'm color blind, the red markers usually appear darker to me."

Andy, the seasoned boater, was beginning to be well seasoned with his diet of liquefied cereal grains.

Again from Andy, "Which way do we go here?"

Ben thinks," I'll live through this, but what time tomorrow morning will I get home?"

How can a 48-minute ride over be converted to a two-hour ride back?

Well, remember, there was the case of deciding where the entrance to the big ditch was.

There was the incident of running straight into a marsh, but thank God for a strong reverse gear on Andy's outboard.

There was the case of the marker whose colored globe, red or green—who knows—had been obviously destroyed by the hurricanes. White lights don't mark channels.

There was the case of meeting a vessel whose green running light was out, its red running light on. That vessel was interpreted to be a red, lighted channel marker.

Never did find out who we almost met —up close and personal.

I did learn that George is a highly religious 'piscopalean. He calls on "Jesus Christ" quite a bit in times of anxiety.

Finally back into the Neuse River, we overshot the unlighted entrance to Dawson's Creek by three miles.

That realization came forth when we could make out the lights of Camp Sea Gull and the state's ferry terminal on the Minnesott side of the Neuse River...Andy, entranced with his depth finder, was reduced to a phonograph playing with a stuck needle.

For all you people who have grown up with nothing but CD's, you'll have to ask your parents about needles sticking on phonograph records.

Anyway, Andy's record kept playing—over and over—"I'm running out of water here. I'm running out of water here. Tell me something. I'm running out of water here."

George, in the most dignified and gentlemanly manner possible, kept requesting Andy to tie up at Ben's dock and call for rides, rather than trying to make way up the small gut up to the wildlife ramp—that is, if Ben's dock could ever be found.

Andy was feeling no fear.

George was deeply concerned.

Ben was beginning to realize that if you were up to your ass in alligators, you should have remembered to drain the swamp. He brilliantly suggested that the boating party stop at his dock on Dawson's Creek long enough to get a flash light to help navigate the small gut up to the boat ramp, that is if they ever made it into Dawson's Creek.

Well they made it to Ben's dock, got the flashlight and headed for the small gut through the woods to the boat ramp.

Ben remembered something that a Marine Patrol

officer had told him about that narrow gut leading to the boat ramp. He didn't share that with the principals in this non-Renoiristic painting of "The Dinner of the Boating Party."

Those citizens from Pairee in Renoir's "Luncheon of the Boating Party" had no need to fear cotton-mouth moccasins dropping from the trees above them into their boat.

It would take too many chapters to describe Andy's use of the flashlight in directing George to back the trailer down the ramp to the boat.

But Ben is so grateful to Andy and George for caring about him—caring enough to venture out at night—in what he later learned was a tricky jour-ney for veterans of high water at high noon—from a back woods boat ramp, across five miles of river, down past the ocean terminal for freighters and oil tankers, to a small seafood restaurant.

Life would be boring without adventure—that is if you don't lose your life?

FIFTY

WHEN WATER COVERED ALL OF THE EARTH

There is sometimes a price to pay for living in a paradise surrounded by water.

Translation—Eastern North Carolina sticks out into the Atlantic Ocean daring hurricanes to strike.

CBS has 48 hours. Here, in the last year of the last millennium, there were 48 days—August 30-October 17, 1999.

First—there was Dennis the Menace.

One of the highlights of Dennis the Menace was wading through water that was armpit deep to get to the steps of the back porch of our studio and gallery.

Jelly fish bites incurred around the navel while

inside a structure are not unheard of—uncommon—but entirely possible.

Meanwhile back at the ranch, water flowed into the house thru the front doors, thru the back door and from the septic tank thru the commode.

It's fairly common to see white caps in the river. On days when there's a right fair wind blow going, white caps can ripple the creek. But when breakers and swells from the creek sweep across the back yard and crash against the house, it's time to go to Plan B, whatever that might be.

Does anybody living landlocked have any idea of the force of hydro-pressure?

But having a studio and a home helps you get not one, but two, Red Cross clean-up kits.

A quart of Clorox—not to mention two quarts—can be a precious commodity.

Richard deCharms brought out his shop vac. Can you imagine trying to vacuum the remnants of the Neuse River?

Ken Brandon strode in the studio when it was past the point of wading in, swung his keys around on that string of his, shrugged his shoulders and mumbled something. Then he came thru with the Hodges Street house and all the ROMEO's (Retired Old Men Eating Out) to help move rusting light stands and a whole lot of other stuff to dry ground.

Andy Polo, Paul Mascara, Doug Daniele and John

Waddell showed up for the move. Richard got there late. Bob Andrews used the excuse that he had to go help Dorothy Whipple trim damaged trees. George Benedict was there in spirit. Ken O'Neil had fled to New York, not afraid of gangsters and muggers, but sent packing by the thought of a little breeze.

Then there was Dennis the Deuce.

Wading out into the yard to retrieve stuff from the back yard that was beginning to float out into the Neuse River across the front yard, the jellyfish again stung more than the bite of the wind.

There was deja vu with that septic tank again. But this time, with the help of two visitors from south of the Rio Grande who took time off from their chores of picking crabmeat, the carpet had been ripped up. That meant less smell.

Oh, with Dennis the Deuce, water went three inches higher in the studio.

Another side bar—Husqvarna riding lawn mowers, no matter how much Paul Harvey ballyhoos about them, are no match for a total submersion in salt water.

Andy Polo changed the English/Italian language trying to get that thing to run again.

And guess what, if you have flood insurance for the house, but not the contents, lawn mowers don't come close to being covered. I don't feel too badly. I wasn't the only one to discover that contents were not covered. After all, living on a virtual island, flood insurance for just the house ain't cheap.

Then there was Floyd.

Other than a golfer, has anybody famous been named Floyd.

Come to think of it, yes. Remember Floyd Patterson?

But, change the "y" to "o" and you have flood instead of Floyd.

Ripped up pieces of carpet were used to sandbag the doors at the house—the outside screen doors. Forgot that rain would blow in thru the screens, flood the front porch and have no way to get out since the screen doors had been sandbagged with mounds of rotting carpet.

But though a tornado ripped down our road and stopped at the house next door, Floyd, with its hundred mile an hour winds for more than hour, hit at an angle that didn't drive the river and the creek to join in the yard around the house.

Of course Floyd's energy was fed by a diet of shingles from the roof.

There followed several applications thru FEMA to the Small Business Administration. Everything but the roll of toilet paper in the studio and the house was faxed to Atlanta.

Also after Floyd, due to the misery upstream, our miserable joke, living completely downstream on the Neuse,—"Having a barbecue this weekend? Then send out a fisherman with a net strong enough to snag pigs and chickens."

And rumor has it that local crabs now have a bacon flavor built in.

Now, Irene.

Emmy purchased a bunch of pillowcases from Family Dollar, 2 for 2 dollars, those with a high polyester content. I had dreamed up the idea that those things filled with sand and tied off with nylon ties would be an excellent version of homemade sand bags.

That really was a good idea, but ...

Irene has come and gone with simply the energy spent putting up and taking everything down again—not to mention sore muscles and a pile of wet sand bags under the car port waiting to either rot in place or be moved.

Needless to say, anchoring down or putting up everything that floats or blows can get to be a chore. Not to mention the un-anchoring and put-ting down.

And there's the matter of the old chain saw that has finally said, "No more. Absolutely no more."

Now the adjuster who was to adjust for the shin-gles devoured by Floyd was scheduled to come the Monday after Irene.

He called to cancel that appointment on the

Sunday afternoon of Irene, after I came home from church to find the living room filling with water dripping from the ceiling because of the loss of shingles for which he had yet visited to adjust for after Floyd.

How's that for a mouth-full?

As a matter of fact, he called right after I had come down from the roof nailing down a tarp in a rainstorm.

My normally, mild mannered self began the conversation with these words, "I am not a happy person."

But what's another hurricane?

Let's see, since July of '96 there's been Bertha, Fran, Bonnie, Dennis the Menace, Dennis the Deuce, Floyd and Irene.

But just think, those last four came in just 48 days of '99.

And as for being stressed, distressed and depressed...

... it seems that there is the possibility that late this afternoon, about the time telemarketers call, somebody from the SBA Disaster Loan department called for Benjamin E. Casey.

Emmy, thinking she smelled a telemarketer, hung up.

Fifty-one

Got A Compass?

Ever been caught up in the "roots" syndrome?

You know there are people who spend vacations searching through cemeteries trying to find family names on headstones, plying through courthouse records looking up deeds, birth and death certificates while interviewing anybody who might have known your great-great-great grandparents or your third cousin fourteen times removed.

This gets to be a fervent endeavor if there is any chance at all that some ancestor was landed gentry, was a politician of note, an inventor, or was the founding father of some town. Find a street named after somebody in your family and, as we say in the

South, "Katie, bar the door."

[Now my wife Emmy, from Buffalo, NY (Yes, Granddaddy, I married a yankee.) says that she had never heard the expression "Katie, bar the door," until I spoke it.

So for others from Buffalo, "Katie, bar the door," is a warning of a big onslaught of something or somebody. That's why you want Katie to bar the door, to keep it or them out. You do understand that back in the days of Daniel Boone, doors didn't have locks. Wooden bars were placed across the door on the inside to keep out any onslaught of unwanted guests.]

And you know there are people who make money, sometimes lots of it, searching your family tree, finding out just who was married to who that somewhere down the line created the two people who created you. I think they are called genealogists.

And when it comes to having forefathers from the old country, wow! Picture frame shops love to see a sentimentalist come in with a coat-of-arms.

As for family trees, I have more sentiment for real trees that some member of my family may have planted. A real tree is real beauty, offering shade and a changing scene every season, unless it's a pine tree which pretty much stays the same, season to season.

Family history is just that, family history.

It's the present that scares me. What have I done with the present? If Abe Lincoln studied by candlelight in a log cabin and became president, why haven't I done better going to good schools that had electric lights?

Some might argue that I'm cynical about all this roots stuff because there are no notable roots that I know of in any trees that make up my family. Well, I take personal pride in knowing who got together to make who in my family but I really am guided by that Abe Lincoln story. What have I made of my life compared to what Abe Lincoln made of his?

It's time to bring about another observation of Robert Fulghum.

Fulghum observed that a compass was more important than a watch...in other words...where we were going was more important than time, and times past.

FIFTY-TWO

DOG DAYS

A re dogs like people?

No.

People are like dogs.

Some dogs wander around all their lives, sniffing out everything from a place to eat to a place to deposit what has been eaten.

Ever watched some dogs just wander about aimlessly—walk a little bit, run a little bit—as if they were trying to figure where they were or where they should be?

Some dogs chase cars and bite tires.

Elusive dreams?

Some dogs sit on the porch and sleep while others never give up the prowl.

I saw a dog today with the definite personality traits that take some of us a half-century to acquire.

This dog was walking along the sidewalk adjacent to the town harbor in Oriental.

His "countenance," as my Mama used to say, told it all.

There was no question. He knew where he was, where he was going and what he was going to do when he got there.

Although I had no idea where he was going or what he was going to do when he got there, it was clear this was a dog clearly focused on the next bone and where it was.

FIFTY-THREE

FELINE REALITY

Daisy, my wonder dog, an adopted greyhound, was sitting at my feet as I scribed the last chapter on the computer.

I rose to go to the dining room table for a break.

Daisy rose to follow me. She lay at my feet while I did a little editing. I can read a printed page better than I can read a computer screen.

I just came back to the computer.

Daisy rose to follow me. She is at my feet now.

Wouldn't it be wonderful if man could be as good a friend to man as dog is to man? Likewise, wouldn't it be wonderful if man could be as good a friend to dog as dog is to man?

Dog is not deceitful, dog is not two-faced.

Dog does not like you...dog bites you.

Dog likes you...dog is your faithful companion, as long as you feed him.

But man was too complacent, lacking enough gratitude for dog.

And so God created cat, the ultimate reality check.

MAMA ALWAYS SAID,

"The Good Lord up in Heaven knows...etc,...etc..."